The Value of the Person
in the Guahibo Culture

SIL International
International Museum of Cultures

Publication in Ethnography 36

Publications in Ethnography is a series published jointly by SIL International and the International Museum of Cultures. The series focuses on cultural studies of minority peoples of various parts of the world. While most volumes are authored by members of SIL International who have done ethnographic research in a minority language, suitable works by others will also occasionally form part of the series.

Series Editor

Barbara Jean Moore

Volume Editors

C. Henry Bradley
Rhonda Hartell
Nancy Sullivan

Production Staff

Bonnie Brown, Managing Editor
Laurie Nelson, Production Manager
Judy Benjamin, Compositor
Hazel Shorey, Graphic Artist

The Value of the Person in the Guahibo Culture

Marcelino Sosa
Translated by Walter del Aguila

A Publication of
SIL International
and
The International Museum of Cultures

Copies of this and other publications of SIL International may be obtained from:

International Academic Bookstore
SIL International
7500 W. Camp Wisdom Road
Dallas, TX 75236-5699

Voice: 972-708-7404
Fax: 972-708-7433
Email: academic_books@sil.org
Internet: http://www.sil.org

Contents

Prologue ix

Preface xiii

About the Author xv

Part 1 Traditional Economy

1 People of the Plains 3
    Seminomadism 3
    Concept of property 5
    Guahibo society 8

2 Guahibo Economic Resources 17
    Natural resources available to the Guahibos 17
    Seasons of the year 20
    Tools, instruments, and utensils 21

3 Agricultural Production and the Division of Labor 25
    Garden away from the home 25
    Home garden 26

4 Distribution of Goods 29
    Social obligation of helping 29
    Social obligation of sharing 30
    Person's worth determines value of material goods 36
    Value of material goods and services 38
    The way business was conducted 42
    Intertribal and intratribal business relations 46

Part 2 Interference by a Foreign Economic System

5 Introduction of a Foreign Economic System   51
   First products of European origin   51
   White merchants   53
   White settlers   56
   Working to get new things   61
   New crops   62
   Arrival of money   62
   Cattle raising   63
   Reservations   64
   Cooperatives   64
   Communal enterprises   66
   Bilingual teachers and health promoters   68

6 Three Socioeconomic Systems.   69
   Hunting and gathering society   69
   Agricultural peasant society   70
   Money-based society.   71

7 Negative Effects on Guahibo Culture.   73
   Business criteria.   73
   Land ownership   74
   Exploitation of natural resources   76
   Work.   77
   Family responsibilities   78
   Property   79
   Human worth   84
   Socioeconomic bases.   86

8 Problems and Failures Resulting from not Understanding the
   White Man's System   89
   Capitalist system   90
   White man's government.   94
   White man's ideological divisions   98

Part 3 The Direction the Guahibo Community Must Take

9 Developing Understanding 103
   Concientización of the Guahibo people 103
   Concientización of the white people 105

10 Specific Suggestions to the Guahibo People 107
   Business 107
   Land holding 108

Contents

Natural resources 109
Work. 110
Family responsibilities 111
Property 112
School 113
Stores 114
Enterprises 115
Conclusions. 116

Epilogue 117

Appendix 1: Glossary of Spanish and Guahibo Words 121

Appendix 2: Guahibo Poetry 125

References 141

Prologue

During the 25 years I lived in an indigenous community in southern Mexico, I met not a few Indian people who, given the educational opportunities I had had, would have become significant, contributing members of the world's social science community because of their analytical and insightful ways of viewing the world in which they found themselves. Marcelino Sosa appears to be such a person.

Almost fifteen years have passed since Sosa's book The Value of the Person in Guahibo Culture was first published privately in Spanish in Colombia. In it he enunciated in clear terms the contrast between the way a local indigenous culture, the Guahibo, and the way an imported culture, the western Spanish culture of Colombia, value the person and the impact that the dominant culture had on the indigenous culture. It provides an additional clear voice to the increasing cry of marginalized, indigenous communities around the world for justice.

Sosa is a Guahibo, born and raised within the Guahibo community. And at the same time he, through life experiences with members of the contemporary, majority Spanish culture has received a thorough education in life within the larger Colombian Spanish-speaking community. Even though his formal education is limited, he shows a degree of sociological and anthropological sophistication normally not found outside of the academy. This is not to say that he is a polished academician; there are times when this fact shows through, but he provides a clear, insightful, and relatively informed voice (even by western standards) for his people.

Not only is he a Guahibo with an inquiring mind, but he is a leader of the larger Guahibo community, a writer in both Guahibo and Spanish, and an educator within his community. In all of these capacities he has served his people and nation. He has served his community as he has represented his people to state and national executives and governing bodies and presented the views of the national government to his people. These experiences have shaped this man and his perspective.

In this book Sosa has described in somewhat traditional ethnographic terms the life of the Guahibo community as an insider, revealing something of its history, has noted the impact of representatives of Colombian western culture, and has revealed to us in expository fashion his vision for his people and their relationship to their nation. He takes the unenviable task of trying to reach two culturally diverse audiences: Colombians and Guahibos. We, in this English version, are extending that reach to include the wider community of the world, a third audience with much greater diversity. I hope that the reader will take that goal into account and not judge Sosa for any shortcomings that are found in attempting to include this third audience.

The reader will note the effect that his life experiences have had on Sosa's point of view and the way he presents it. The influence of the Spanish language into which this book was first written is apparent on every page and we have not obliterated that artifact of the original version.

This original essay falls into three parts: a description of traditional economy, interference by a foreign economic system, and a polemic for the future development of the Guahibo community.

In the first part of the book Guahibo culture is described in terms of its people and their society, their economic resources and technology, their agricultural production and division of labor, and the distribution of goods and services among them. The key ingredient of production and distribution in this society, Sosa claims, is the social obligation of reciprocal helping and sharing.

In the second part of the book he focuses on ways in which the national Colombian economic system intruded and disrupted the local Guahibo economic system. The first impact of European intrusion was through its products, both natural and manufactured. Then its agents arrived in the forms first of traveling merchants and later of permanent settlers. They brought along with them a different perspective on life including different agricultural crops, animals, and medium of exchange—money. Ultimately, this different way of life led to reservations, cooperatives, bilingual education, and health promoters for the Guahibos.

The blending of the third way of subsistence reflecting a money-based economy with the mixed system of hunting and gathering and incipient agriculture led to cultural and social stresses that stretched the Guahibo way of life in uncontrollable ways. The negative effects of these incommensurate systems was and is seen in contrasting ideas of land ownership, exploitation of natural resources, work, property, family relationships and responsibilities, and one's sense of human worth. Mutual understanding was difficult, if not impossible, to reach between the indigenous people and those who intruded into their homeland.

In the third part of the book Sosa suggests some directions the Guahibos might take in a proactive way in order to confront the problems they face. The first step is to increase their own understanding of their situation by raising their level of consciousness. The second step calls for interaction with the larger Spanish-speaking population in an effort to help its members to raise their level of consciousness with respect to the Guahibos. In this way the Guahibos will be able to position themselves to reverse the destructive trend in which they find themselves and to find themselves in this larger world. He touches on the topics of business, land holding, natural resources, work, family responsibilities, property, school, and stores and makes specific comments about becoming bicultural in their attempt at preserving their own culture but at the same time striving to become participants in the culture of their nation and to inform its members of the importance and significance of their culture.

In the Epilogue we see Sosa as a pragmatist, rather than an idealist, in recording the developments of the last fifteen years and detailing the achievements of the Guahibo with their Spanish-speaking neighbors and the national government. Although the results of their efforts are somewhat different from the results he proposed in 1985, he recognizes that they are significant and are moving in an appropriate direction. However, many of his suggestions have taken place. He sees the road into the future as rocky but traversible.

Sosa's approach here has been experiential along with a modicum of appropriate research. He builds his narrative not just on his own experiences in his village, in local towns, and in the capitol city—Bogotá—but also on those of his relatives and other compatriots particularly with regard to knowledge, experiences, and events of the relatively recent past. He includes information about the region by citing relevant written sources—both historical and contemporary—to include information with which he does not have first-hand experience. Furthermore, he appears to build his case in a direct and penetrating way and as fairly and honestly as could be attained by one who has experienced the events of his life and of his fellow Guahibos.

Sosa's purpose is to make a positive contribution to his cultural group and to his nation. There is no question that Sosa, his immediate and extended family, and his fellow Guahibos have suffered many indignities and traumas over the past, but there is no evidence of that in his writing except for a modest, direct accounting of those experiences. He even provides an even-handed, first-person account of human rights violations that he and his family suffered, yet without animosity and bitterness. Although this work is not a precise and complete blueprint of his vision, it includes enough analysis of and insight into problems his people face and enough detail to serve as a guide for the future for the Guahibo community and local and federal governmental entities in addressing the many problems that still exist for this community. There will continue to be problems at the interface between it and the national society of which it is a part, as there are problems between all communities within any nation regardless of its degree of homogeneity and similarity. Nevertheless, the program he outlines has made a strong first step toward a positive future for all concerned.

Herein lies the significance of this book. It should help local, state, and national leaders understand the plight of the Guahibo people from their perspective, it should animate the Guahibos themselves to continue to form their own solutions to the multiple social, economic, and political problems they face, and it should be considered an example demonstrating what can be accomplished for marginalized groups not just in Colombia but around the world.

C. Henry Bradley, December 1999

Preface

In the eastern plains of our beautiful Republic of Colombia, we, an Indian nation, the Guahibo community, live. We have been the object of many studies. That is, our socioeconomic problems have been studied by government officials (Ministry of Government, DAINCO, Colombian Agrarian Reform Institute (INCORA), etc.) and by university students. The author, as a member of the Guahibo society, seeing things from the Indian viewpoint, wants to make his small contribution by means of this study. He offers his knowledge to orient first the white investigator and second the Guahibo and other interested Indians.

In the plains the word "white" is used to refer to a non-Indian person (without any racist intention), and in this book the author will use it in that sense (non-Indian Colombian), and "white culture" in referring to the corresponding culture, that is, the majority culture of Colombia.

Due to the ever-increasing penetration of this majority culture, and especially its economic system, our Guahibo culture has suffered a very great shock. In this author's opinion, the economic system the Guahibos had before was much better than the white man's system since the Guahibo economy was based on the value of human beings. In order to understand this view, the reader will have to try to put himself in our situation as Guahibos who believe that it is not things that give value to the individual, but it is rather the individual who makes things valuable. Then the reader will easily understand how the Guahibo Indians viewed values in their culture and will know the extreme shock that our Guahibo people are suffering today.

For this understanding to happen, it is necessary to know the historical process of penetration by the white economic system into the Guahibo society. For that reason some points will be mentioned, explaining who the agents of change were. First, though, it is necessary to analyze the orientation and the mechanism of the traditional Guahibo economy prior to the arrival of the whites.

Three historic periods of Guahibo economy and social life will be described: (1) the time prior to knowing the white economic system and its industrial products; (2) the time when Guahibos began to know money and its value and the disorientation it caused, even though their own system remained more or less stable; and finally, (3) the more recent times when they came to find out that money is the main means to acquire things and at the same time to undervalue people, to separate them from one another, to cause hatred, and even to bring people to the point where they prefer getting money above respecting human life itself. They prefer having money to a peaceful life, such as the Guahibos had before the arrival of this system.

Now the Guahibos have the problem of not knowing how to choose the way to go amid internal and external conflicts, and all of us must help them as thinking human beings.

Acknowledgments

The author would like to thank Dr. Steve Walter, Trina Kondo, and all the people who encouraged him to write this book and supported him with their suggestions; the financial aid from the Agency for International Development (AID) from Alberta Province, Canada; the elderly Guahibos who told him about history, especially his aunt Mercedes and his uncle Rafael, and Sussy Orozco, who checked the spelling and helped with the typing. The author assumes all responsibility for the ideas herein expressed.

About the Author

Marcelino Sosa was born in 1938, in Murure (now a ranch), on the banks of the Manacacías River, near Puerto Gaitán, Meta, Colombia. During the period of violence (1949–1953) he lived with his father near the Casibare Creek rain forests. Casibare Creek is a tributary of the Manacacías River. There his father, against his own will, had to give shelter to Dumar Aljure and his band of armed men for a few days, for which he suffered the Colombian army's reprisal. All of this violence made a strong impression on the children, and the Guahibo families were forced to flee the Manacacías River region. The author's family moved on to the Planas River region.

From the age of twelve the author had to work for some periods of time at the Candilejas ranch, in haciendas on the Pajure River and in Puerto López. During that time he started to investigate, asking questions of various people and analyzing why things were so. It was there he learned to read and write.

He was living with his relatives in San Rafael de Planas in 1970 when the armed incident known as *Jaramillera* took place, a very widely publicized case. During that period he suffered very much, together with many Guahibo families.

Afterwards, in 1973, he moved east into the San José de Ocuné region. There, in 1978, he was elected captain of captains for the Cavasi Creek Reservation. After his resignation from this position two years later, he became the reservation coordinator. He was a councilman for the Vichada Territory during two periods—one by designation in the Turbay Ayala presidency and the second one by popular election as substitute for Efraín Azhavache. He was also captain of the Macocová village up to the time of his appointment as magistrate of San José de Ocuné, the largest jurisdiction within the Vichada. He served one year in that position and then resigned in order to give more time to his people and to write.

In 1978, the author founded *La Voz del Cavasi*, the first Guahibo-Spanish bilingual periodical, which he continues to manage. He wrote his first essay entitled "El Guahibos y el blanco: Culturas en conflicto," which received first prize in the essay category in the first contest on applied anthropology among Colombian Indian societies in 1980. This was sponsored by the General Direction for Community Integration and Development of the Colombian Ministry of Government. His second essay, "El niño Guahibo y la educación bilingüe," was published in 1983. "Between Two Worlds," a documentary video, was based on this essay. His third essay, "El valor de la persona en la economía Guahibo," was written in 1984, and it demonstrates the importance given to personal worth in the traditional Guahibo economic system and the shock Guahibos experienced at the introduction of an economy based on other values.

The author was the first director of the Guahibo Committee for Integral Bilingual Education, an organization in which he continues serving today.

Part 1

Traditional Economy

1

People of the Plains

To the Guahibos, people of the plains, social relations were a very important economic factor: in their kind of work, in the distribution of goods, and in dealing with other Indians. That is why it is important to have some understanding of Guahibo life and of their social organization in order to comprehend their traditional economic system.

The elderly Guahibos of the Vichada River valley remember when the first white people came into their region. The description offered here is based primarily on what they remember and on what their parents and grandparents told them. Some stories written in the 18th century by Jesuit priests (Gumilla, Rivero, and others) were also consulted. The description is that of the Guahibos who lived (and still live) in the region of the Vichada River and its tributaries and not of the groups of the same linguistic family who live in the districts of Arauca and Casanare (Cuibas, Masiguares, Macaguanes, etc.) and along the Guaviare River and its tributaries.

The Guahibos think of themselves as people of the plains, even though they always had their homes near the rain forests where they could plant their gardens. They lived in small villages of about five to thirty houses; they were subsistence farmers and also lived by hunting, fishing, and gathering.

Seminomadism

The Guahibos have always been seminomadic as far as it was possible to ascertain by talking to the older Guahibos. They used to plant their

3

gardens of manioc and corn together with plantains, sugar cane, pineapple, sweet potatoes, and other plants, but on some occasions and for some reasons would go out from their villages and into other regions. This author has previously written about this seminomadism (Sosa 1979) but will briefly mention some reasons here.

1. In the summertime the Guahibos would leave their homes and go to various places because traveling was easier that time of the year. Since the land was dry, rivers and creeks could be crossed without any problem, due to their shallowness. On such occasions, the Guahibos would go out on long hikes with all their families to spear fish in the shallow lakes, play with the family on the beaches, gather turtle eggs, etc. By no means did they abandon their houses because the Guahibos always came back to their homes and to their gardens. In the winter the Guahibos were more sedentary due to the hard rains; the deep creeks and rivers made travel impossible.
2. It was also the case that whenever an epidemic of any kind would break out, the Guahibos would either retire to some other place, leaving their homes and gardens temporarily, or they would move elsewhere to avoid a bad epidemic.
3. The Guahibos would also move out to some other place in order to attend religious activities or to take a sick person to the shaman.
4. When they saw that the game or the good land to raise manioc was becoming scarce, they would also move out to some other place.
5. A Guahibo found leaving for another village easy when he had a relative in the new place, be it a relative of the man or of the woman. Such a visit would last one month, or even years, if the relatives did not want him to go back.

So for these and perhaps other reasons it could be said that the Guahibos were a seminomadic people. The chronicles of the conquerors and of the Jesuit priests of the sixteenth, seventeenth, and eighteenth centuries tell that the Guahibos, speakers of the Guahibo language family who inhabited the northern Casanare region, were more nomadic. Gumilla (1955), in fact, called them "gipsies." They did not plant gardens, but lived only by hunting, fishing, and gathering and had less durable houses or huts.

In contrast, toward the northwest the conquerors found permanent towns of agricultural Guahibos (Kirchoff 1948; del Rey Fajardo 1971:27). In this book we will be referring to this latter group, whom the author believes to be the one now living in the region of the Vichada River and its tributaries. This group has assimilated many Sáliba, Achagua, Piapoco, and Cabere Indians.

Concept of property

In order to understand the traditional Guahibo economic system, it is important to understand our concept of property. The Guahibos recognize two main kinds of property: collective and individual. But these concepts are different from those of the whites. As it has been explained in previous writings (Sosa 1979 and 1983), the Guahibos considered all nonmanmade things, such as sunshine, breeze, rain, land, rivers, creeks, lakes, and trees in the forests, to be collective or public property. The land, with its plains, rain forests, trees, etc., belonged to whoever exploited it, the same as the rivers, brooks, and lakes with their fish and other edible species. No Guahibo would ever think, "This is my pond, my segment of brook, my beach, my plain." All these things belonged to everybody living in the land, to all who would work them.

The Guahibos also had the concept of individual or personal property. The author considers best to call it *individual* property rather than *private* property for reasons that will be explained later. Things made by a Guahibo person were individual property—his house, his garden, his bow and arrows, etc. Bought things were in the same category—his dog, his axe, his hat. But a Guahibo would always place such things at the service of society, for the good of all.

For instance, a Guahibo had his house which was his own property because he (perhaps with a son or a son-in-law) had built it, but that did not mean that someone else could not use it. A house was built for personal use and, whenever necessary, for collective use as well, always with a sense of solidarity with those who for various reasons had no house. It was more common to share a house with other relatives, but if someone else not related to the family did not have a house, he would also be welcome.

Another example, a Guahibo always had his bow and arrows (essential for the family's daily provisions) made through his own work for his own personal use. But if another Guahibo wanted to go hunting, the first one would lend the bow and arrows to him unselfishly. Borrowing a bow, however, was not a very common thing to do, since usually everybody had his own because it was an indispensable item in the economy. If it had to be done, the owner himself would be very happy knowing that what he had was being useful to someone else. Even in the absence of the owner, whoever needed the bow and arrows could take them, the only condition being that he let the owner know that he had taken them in his absence; thus, everything was fine. In some cases, a more timid person would not take a lesser known person's arrows, but in any event the owner would not complain.

For another example, a Guahibo would buy a dog which would be his personal property, but whatever game the dog caught was for almost everybody who lived in the village. On some occasions the neighbors would come to the dog's owner and invite him to go along on a hunting trip, so he would take the dog along, and afterwards, whatever game was obtained was distributed among them all.

Some personal property belonged to the men—bows and arrows, an axe, a machete, a miner's pick, his personal hammock, etc. Other property belonged to the women—fishing net, cooking pots, her own personal hammock, etc. But borrowing someone else's personal things was always acceptable and very common. One could even ask to borrow a man's hat when going on a trip under the hot sun.[1]

Trails to personal gardens, bridges, and ports also were personal property because they had been made by one person (or by several members of one family), even though they could not be taken home. All these nontransportable personal possessions were at the service of society without ever showing selfishness. The reason for such things being available for everybody is that, since the land was not divided, any member of the group could use the trail, the bridge, or the lakes because there was no regulation for such things.

The Guahibos had almost no private property[2] and did not know such a concept, the only exception being the shamans. They had some private property related to magic, but shared their other (individual) property, for instance, the house, like any other Guahibo. To function well as shamans, they had certain objects, regulations, and secrets they shared only with others of their own profession.

The white man's concept of private property was foreign to the Guahibos. The author remembers his relatives asking him as contact with the neocolonial started, "Why do the white men put padlocks on the gates when they fence up their farms? Is it to make a distinction between whites and Guahibos?" I would answer them saying that it was the whites' custom because they consider a farm to be private property, a piece of land where they have some things, and so they think that they are the only ones who should have access to the enclosed land, and besides, they also have some other things for the owner's private use, such as his house, the

---

[1]The author's aunt tells about the time when clothes made by white people were still very scarce, how people needing to travel to Orocué on business would borrow clothes for the trip from those who had them.

[2]Here and elsewhere the author uses the term "private property" in its legal sense. That is to say, an owner of private property has the right to use the property, its derivatives and profits; to hold it in possession; to abuse and destroy it if he so wishes; to prohibit its use by others; and to defend it, to even kill another person who trespasses his home without his consent.

room where he sleeps, his car, his dog, etc. The white man thinks that all such things are his legitimate property, with no one else having the right to make use of them. Not even a friend can use one's private property without the owner's permission. He could legally denounce his friend for abuse of trust. Furthermore, a white man has the right to not use his property or to destroy it if he finds it convenient to do so. But as I would explain this matter to them they would smile, as the concept could not enter their minds. Perhaps only the shamans understood it to some extent since they also had some things for their private use in magic and healing, they being the only ones who knew how to use them.

The white man also has the concept of collective property, but it is different from the Guahibo concept. It includes all things found in the cities belonging to the state (that is, a people with its greater and lesser "chiefs" who constitute the government)—streets and roads, bridges, schools, water system, and other public services under government management. It is called collective property because all of it has the purpose of serving the citizens who contribute their taxes to the government to pay for maintenance, repairs, administrators' salaries, etc.

Within a group of white people some things can also be owned in common, such as a house, a business, a car, a boat. Even though it is for the benefit of all, however, it is also private property because the services and rights are only for the associates, and they are the only ones who can vary the programs by common consent. The Guahibo finds this type of association hard to understand, because he has never had this kind of organization. Guahibos never had a piece of communal property that needed to be administered or maintained, such as a school, for example. All this kind of property, because it did not belong to nature, was individual property and the individual's responsibility. That is to say, a company or a cooperative car would, in the Guahibo concept, be very much private property because it is not loaned to just anyone who needs it. At the same time, it would be very much communal property because the care for it would be the responsibility of a group (a concept that did not exist), rather than of an individual.[3]

Since they did not have collective property that needed to be administered, they did not need a government that would group several families. Each village had its own leader whom they later called "captain", but there were no chiefs for an entire region or community (tribe). That is why they did not understand the organization concept.

---

[3]We can mention here another subclass of Guahibo individual property: family property. Guahibos consider a house and a garden as family property (a man's and his wife's.) See also footnote 6, chapter 3.

Guahibo society

Our Guahibo society is based on the relationships between different family members. In order to understand how the traditional economic system functioned, it is necessary to understand how the family functioned.

Excerpting from an earlier essay (Sosa 1983:10),

> part of the value of a family is the Guahibo concept of respect. The Guahibo language has two words meaning 'to respect': *yáiyatane* has a meaning similar to that of the Spanish word used in reference to those in authority, such as parents, adults, teachers, patrons, the president, etc. The other word is *urátane* shows respect based on special values and norms in Guahibo culture, such as in relations with parents-in-law, siblings of the opposite sex, etc. So, for instance, a Guahibo father must not kiss his own daughter if she is older than five, because besides loving her he must respect her *(urátane)* because she is of the opposite sex. The same is true of a mother and her son; they cannot even walk together by themselves, because if they did so, they would be breaking the rules of Guahibo culture. A Guahibo person must also respect *(urátane)* his/her parents-in-law, parents, and siblings of both sexes. He/she must not scold them nor joke around with them, especially about sex. *urátane* is an intimate kind of respect, and not to show it when one should is a very shameful thing.

Parent-children relationship. The Guahibo couple (father and mother) maintained a constant (daily) relationship with all their children living at home. This characteristic was true of both father and mother. The relationships with the younger children were closer. Both father and mother would protect the child. They would take him/her in their arms, cuddle him/her, and thus the child would keep on growing. At the same time the father or the mother would guide him/her so that he/she would learn to relate affectionately and respectfully to his own younger siblings and other relatives of his/her parents. Parents would take advantage of their children's infancy to instill in their minds respect and solidarity toward their fellow human beings, without any selfish feelings. But as the children would grow up, the parents would become more and more detached from them but without ever failing to teach them the values of their society.

When the boy or girl reached the age of seven or eight, the relationship to the parents would start to change; now the relations were according to gender. The father would relate more closely to the son and the mother to her daughter. Among Guahibos the relationships were always gender-based. Spouses were the only ones who could relate very closely, except for some special cases.

Relationship between in-laws. A son-in-law and his father-in-law maintained a very respectful (*urátane*) relationship. The son-in-law could accept teaching from his father-in-law; they could travel, go hunting and fishing together, by themselves or in the company of others. He could not do the same with his mother-in-law, however, being of the opposite sex. The mother-in-law would relate more closely to her son's wife. It was not looked on well if a son-in-law would spend much time with his mother-in-law, engage in long conversations with her, or the two should walk together unaccompanied. The same would apply to the father-in-law and his son's wife. These norms were extended to the society in general.

The young son-in-law's duty was to be able to perform all the chores his father-in-law had to do (everything a man in Guahibo society did) without having to be so ordered by the father-in-law nor having to ask him how to do them, although sometimes he—very much embarrassed—would ask out of necessity

The daughters-in-law had the same relationship with their mothers-in-law, and many times the obligatory suggestions were made through the women. The mother would tell the daughter that the father had some manioc to be planted. If the son-in-law had not heard it, the daughter would repeat the message to her husband, and, thus, the father-in-law would indirectly give orders and still keep a respectful relationship with his son-in-law.

When the son-in-law had little inclination to be helpful with the household chores, hunting, and fishing, the mother-in-law would be the first one to intervene in letting the son-in-law know his responsibility to help in the work. She would first advise the daughter, very formally without the son-in-law realizing it, that he should help the father-in-law with a certain job. If the girl told her husband and he did not pay attention to her, then the mother-in-law, now angrily, would tell the daughter in the son-in-law's presence, that he should be ashamed (*aura*) of himself and help his father-in-law work or do whatever was necessary to support a wife.

If, in spite of that, he still did not listen, then the father-in-law would call the son-in-law and would kindly give him orders, and then if he did not obey, the father-in-law could speak to him angrily; the young man was no longer worthy of living with the daughter. If a son-in-law did not work for his father-in-law, he was considered incapable to fulfill his family responsibilities and did not deserve to have a wife. He was a bad son-in-law who, due to his own laziness, was not capable of supporting a family.

The same was true for the daughter-in-law with regards to the mother-in-law. It was almost the same as the case of the son-in-law and the father-in-law.

Since it was expected that the son-in-law, a married man, should help the father-in-law more than his own father, it was always advantageous for a man to have several daughters and not only sons.

Relationship among siblings. Such relations were permanent and good, but they had to be among siblings of the same gender. They all could get together, but a male would prefer to be with his sister's husband, and the women would gather in a group apart.

Relationship among cross-cousins. Among cross-cousins (children of the father's sister, or of the mother's brother), they could relate with those of the opposite sex, since a young man could marry one of these female cousins. Parents always preferred their sons to marry within the family, and the young girls' parents felt the same way.

Relationship among parallel-clousins. Parallel-cousins could not intermarry because they were considered legitimate siblings. These cousins respected *(urátane)* one another though they also were very close friends. Among the male cousins of this type they would not treat one another as brothers-in-law, but rather as brothers, while the male cross-cousins on both sides would treat each other as brothers-in-law, even though they did not live with their sisters. In Guahibo, the same label is used for cross-cousin and for brother-in-law *(támojo)*.

Relationship between a nephew and his "uncle-father." The nephew's relation to his uncle-father (father's brother or husband of mother's sister) was similar to the son-father relationship. This uncle felt responsible for caring for the nephew in the absence of his father, as well as for his niece, although the niece related more closely to her aunt. The name for this uncle is the same as for step-father *(taxúanë)*.

Relationship between a nephew and his "uncle-father-in-law." The relationship between these two also was very close, but in this case the nephew-son-in-law always treated his uncle-father-in-law (mother's brother or husband of father's sister) with special deference *(urátane)*. A nephew-son-in-law was almost ashamed to have to ask his uncle-father-in-law something he did not know about work, because he was the father of the girls he might eventually marry.

Relationship between sweethearts from the same village. A young nephew-son-in-law would frequently visit the home of his uncle-father-in-law to seek a close relationship and gradually overcome his shyness before the whole family. In such visits the young man would frequently help his uncle-father-in-law in all his chores, as well as go hunting and fishing with him, or by himself, in order to bring something to his uncle-father-in-law's home.

The two young people would have long chats about how they were going to behave and about the responsibilities towards each other and in their family. If during such conversations they did not reach an agreement, they could break relations, although this situation would very seldom happen, since the girl's parents were her advisors. If the young man was lazy, that would give the prospective parents-in-law and bride sufficient grounds to reject him.

During that period the young man would propose to the young woman (his cross-cousin) and find out if she would accept him as her husband or not. Normally, the girl would not accept a proposal without her parent's consent

If the girl's parents saw that he had a good head on his shoulders and was capable of supporting his wife and children later on, they both loved each other, and there was no objection from any other relatives, the parents would authorize the girl to start becoming friendly with the young man, perhaps going along with him to his place of work, or on a fishing trip, etc.

When the time for the union would come, no religious rite was customary nor would anything special be done for the young couple, nor for the parents-in-law. After the couple was united, the man would go live in the girl's family home so he could always help the father-in-law. Again, this action was subject to the girl's consent; otherwise, there was nothing the young man could do.

Relationship between sweethearts from different villages. Guahibo young men got married between 18 and 22 years of age. Girls could get married after their first menstrual period. When the young man was from a different village, he would leave his own town and move into the home of the parents whose daughter he hoped to marry, bringing his own personal effects and arrows. Then he would start helping the girl's father in his chores, and fishing and hunting until he and the girl, as well as the parents, became better acquainted. Then he would propose to the girl. If the girl and her parents agreed, the young man would remain in the family and assume the same responsibilities of marriage.

Relationship between spouses. A married couple could live for a while in the father-in-law's home. When they started having children, the husband had to build their own house. It was then when the man would start distancing himself from his obligations in the father-in-law's home, although he would always have to help from time to time. Now it was his main duty to build the house, plant his own garden, and make all the things his wife would need, such as the backpack to carry manioc, a sieve, and many other types of baskets and implements needed for food preparation and storage.

Divorce existed among the Guahibo people, but it was not very common. It would happen whenever a married couple could not get along in their daily lives. For instance, if the woman was too crazy, lazy, sickly, or sterile, or if her family interfered in their home life. Or if the husband was lazy and did not fulfill his home obligations, did not know how to do anything, or his own family made his life with that woman impossible, etc., they could divorce. If that was the case, the separation could be arranged between the couple, without much difficulty, since after the separation each one was free to establish a union with whomever he/she wanted. If they had any children, they would reach an agreement about who would keep them, without ever neglecting to visit the children who stayed with the other parent. The one keeping the children would not prohibit the other parent to ever see them. Many times the children would stay with either set of grandparents. In such cases, both sets of grandparents would reach an agreement as to who would keep the children. Separation was easier when the couple had no children; once having children, it is difficult for a Guahibo man to separate from his wife, because of his love for his children. Besides, a Guahibo man loved his wife very much because she was the mother of those who would take care of him in the future. That is why Guahibo men would try not to leave their wives alone for a long time. A Guahibo man who left his wife alone for a long time was not a good husband; he had to stay home to direct the home education of his children. To maintain good relations in the home, the man would grant many rights to the wife, such as taking care of the garden at harvest time, distributing the game catch among other members of the family, taking care of her home, and sharing her own ideas with him. In order to have a good home there had to be good mutual understanding between husband and wife and also among all relatives on both sides.

The step-father and his duties. When a husband died, and there were children, and if the woman remarried, the new husband was obligated to care for his wife's children. He would enter into the category of uncle-father (with that title), as if he were a brother of the dead father. By no means were the children left abandoned. The same applied in the event that a divorced woman should remarry.

The grandfather. The grandfather directed family relationships on a higher and broader level. He gave counsel to all his grandchildren as to their relationships with the rest of society. As a result of this, generally, the grandfather would keep well aware of all that was going on in the family. The grandmother had similar authority though somewhat less than the grandfather.

It was the grandfather who related to the other grandfathers in the village to give his opinion on matters that needed their attention. The grandfathers related to the other villages more than the others to interchange ideas, conduct business, and to know the family ties among Guahibos in all the region. For various social and economic aspects of community life, it was important to know all the family relationships—who even the most distant cousins were and what kind of cousins they were, etc.

Many times the grandfather was the chief (later on the captain) or the shaman (or both) in a town, and it was expected that he would apply all his knowledge on behalf of the family and all of society. He was the chief who would call on the chief of another village to plan a great fishing trip for the two groups, or a work project, or only to take some good or bad news to him. If he was a shaman, he would visit another shaman to inhale *yopo* and chat with him about his secret science and exchange news or old stories. Sometimes both the chief and the shaman would go together because they got along very well.

Relationship among relatives living far from one another. Guahibos kept in touch with the most remote members of their extended families, and because of this, they had relatives scattered throughout the entire Guahibo territory. Guahibos held the view that all of them belonged to the same family and sought to establish family ties even with every unknown person.

These relatives that Guahibos had in distant towns were individuals or entire families who in times past had moved away, perhaps taking a sick family member to the shaman, or as the result of fighting among them, or just to visit a relative. These long-distance relatives were those who, upon learning the news and plans of those in their town, took it upon themselves to carry such news to their family or tell them whenever they came to visit. They always extended hospitality to visiting relatives. When coming to visit a relative, the guests took advantage of the opportunity for getting to know other relatives of the host, who also ended up being the visitor's relatives. It was advantageous having relatives in all places, because one could stay in their homes when traveling.

Relationship among merchants *(wijá).*[4] Other people who always kept in touch with one another, without necessarily being relatives, were the merchants. Those interested in business had other people with similar interests with whom they traded things. They traveled to different villages, sometimes very distant from one another, taking things to trade with their clients *(wijanë)*, who would welcome them warmly. The client then would have to travel in order to return the visit and to exchange other things, collect a bill, etc.

These people had a very special and respectful relationship among themselves. They were people with the same interests who developed a very special kind of friendship (like brothers). They appreciated the effort that their client made in coming to visit them because they knew the trails, the difficulties, and the long distance between the villages. So they sought to treat their client the best way possible, looking for ways to please him through good care and the good things he would get from them.

Relationship among Guahibos from different villages and rivers. Relationships among villages were constant due to various reasons—family relations, to visit traditional shamans, to attend festivities, and for business. Travel was on foot using the trails joining the villages or, less frequently, by river in canoes. There were main trails that would follow along the rivers running from the headwaters down to the mouth of the river. These trails would pass through rain forests and streams. Rivers were used for the same purpose, especially when the whole family would travel. There also were trails between rivers (running from north to south mainly) for the purposes of social interaction between people from different rivers.

---

[4]In order to facilitate the pronunciation of Guahibo words, accent marks have been used according to Spanish language rules, though accents are not used in writing for Guahibo speakers. The syllable is not accented in Guahibo, but the word *wijá* ends in a long vowel, which causes it to sound stressed. The sixth vowel *(ë)* is pronounced as 'u' but without rounding the lips (smiling). *th* is an aspirated *t*. A tilde over a vowel means the vowel is nasalized.

Certainly, the people from closely neighboring villages had more social interaction. Such villages would overlap some, forming something like a chain of interrelated peoples along the rivers.

Based on Guahibo accounts, the author surmises that the Guahibos were divided according to rivers, such as the people from Tomo River *(tomopijiwi)*, those from the Vichada River *(witsarapijiwi)*, those from the Muco River *(mucopijiwi)*, those from the Plana River *(planapijiwi)*, those from the Guaviare River *(wawialipijiwi)*, etc. Groups from one river had most of their interaction with others from the same river. To the north, the Cuiba, Masiguare groups, and others of the same Guahibo linguistic family (but who were more namadic) would each travel on a particular river, which was considered their own.

The visits made by Guahibos would extend from a few days into weeks and even into years, depending on circumstances, family ties, and the visitors' wishes. Guahibos thought it very important to tend to guests, regardless of how long they stayed. It was always a pleasure to entertain guests and it was no trouble to stay home with them, even when one had other things to do. Guahibo people always found it important to exchange ideas in conversation and would have long chats regardless of the time they would take. This hospitality was a demonstration of esteem, familiarity, and a sense of cordiality and human solidarity. Dialogue has always been an important aspect of friendship. Generally, following the initial greetings conversations were very funny, full of joking and laughter among groups of the same sex and age. The women, the young people, and the adult men would separate to be able to chat more intimately about things of special interest to each group. This form of social interaction also was a way of catching up on the news. Guahibos had neither radios nor newspapers to spread the news.

To give the reader an idea of how the Guahibo society was formed by family groups in each region, mainly along the rivers, figure 1 shows how the family groups were interlocked. In that way small groups would form a very large family that included all the Guahibo-speaking community in which everybody cared for one another in all aspects of social life.

Figure 1. Model of interlocking family groups

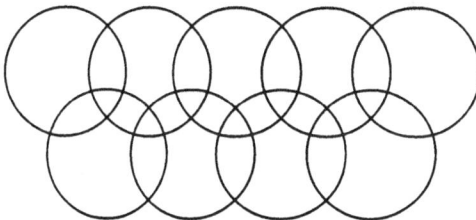

2

Guahibo Economic Resources

Our Guahibo ancestors gathered all they needed for daily living from their natural environment—food, shelter, clothing (tree bark or cotton fiber), ornaments, etc. Initially, all their tools were homemade, using natural regional materials.

Natural resources available to the Guahibos

The land occupied by the Guahibos was divided into plains, clusters of vegetation along rivers and lakes, and forests. The rivers and streams were used for fishing.

The Guahibos had a very advanced concept about the land. Not that they worshiped "mother earth" in a mystical way, but they understood very well that the earth was the basis for everything and gave life to all. As we mentioned earlier, they considered the land to be (by nature) the common property of all human beings. This concept was universally shared by all Guahibos. They never thought otherwise.

Exploitation of the land. The Guahibo people used the land for many purposes. They hunted for wild animals of many kinds—tapir, armadillo, etc. They gathered palm fruits and other types of fruit, and extracted oil from some of them. They used woods of all kinds, including palm bark, to build their houses, some furniture (cabinets, shelves, and benches), and tools (bows and arrows, etc.). Palm leaves were used for roofing, basket weaving, and as a source of fiber for weaving hammocks. The forests were

17

also a source for resins of various kinds (used as adhesives), roots whose juice was used for fishing, vines and tree bark used for tying things together, and medicinal herbs.

The woods and forests would be slashed and burned to plant manioc and other crops. Various kinds of wild and cultivated cane were used to make baskets, flutes, and arrows. Dyes were extracted from tree bark, fruits, and leaves; certain kinds of clay were used for pottery-making; bees-wax was used as a glue and for candles; gourds were used to make spoons and cups; and the bark of certain trees was used to make garments, bags, and baby straps (for carrying). And there were many other products.

The plains were good hunting grounds for deer, armadillo, and other species, and for gathering edible roots and medicinal herbs. The woods and forests were used for agriculture but never as places to live. Houses were always built in the plains, near rivers and streams.

Extension of exploited land. Each Guahibo man cultivated from one to one-and-a-half hectares of land per year to support his family. The women would replant the field as they harvested manioc, so the land was used two or three consecutive years. Then the land was allowed to rest for three or four years (if it was fertile) before planting again. After this last harvest, the land would be allowed to rest for five or six years. Otherwise, the land would yield less (smaller manioc) and produce too many weeds. The Guahibos used the land in a way that did not require weeding.

Guahibos always liked to have an abundance of meat. The larger the unpopulated area, the more game it would provide. Often the Guahibos would leave their villages and go hunting and fishing in a more isolated place. This journey would take up to a week's time.

Guahibo houses were built using a specially durable kind of wood for posts. The thatch roofs were preferably of *moriche* palm leaves, because they were more durable than other kinds. The *chuapo* palm wood was used for the roof frame as well as some furniture, and sometimes for the house walls. The roofs and walls made of these materials lasted about five years. If the town was big or if there were only a few palm patches available, the palm leaves would become scarce after all the houses had been roofed twice. So after ten years or so, it was necessary to relocate the village so people did not have to go too far to gather palm leaves.

The same was the case when other things such as game, productive land, etc., were depleted. All this resource depletion made it necessary for the Guahibos to hold large extensions of land.

Sometimes the entire town would relocate, or frequently small groups of people would gradually move out. Due to this movement and other reasons already mentioned (see the section on seminomadism in chapter 1) the town's population was variable.

It is hard to estimate the extent of land a family or a community needed for all its activities in planting, gathering, hunting, and fishing, but Eden explains the difficulties caused by not knowing the required resources.

> Even humanitarian contacts with Indians have had wide-ranging and sometimes harmful effects upon the Indian culture. Frequently these effects come about for lack of understanding the intimate relationship existing between socioeconomic patterns and resources available in tribal areas. Thus, for instance, even marginal invasions into apparently vacant Indian land, can cause a food shortage, due to the traditional way of gathering it, which requires a larger extension of land. Likewise, problems can result from the concentration of Indian settlements around installations for newly introduced services, such as stores or mission schools, which bring about local pressure upon the land and natural resources. Furthermore, the provision of health services, resulting in population growth, could cause a higher food demand exceeding the capacity of the available land to provide it by traditional methods. Even when alternate means of subsistence are offered, such as, for instance, work for daily wages, the abandoning of traditional subsistence activities could lead to an impoverished low-level assimilation into a money-based economy in which nutrition and health are at a risk. (Eden 1974)

Coppens, calculating a longer period of time than the author does for the land to be reconstituted, and without figuring in "demographic growth and sociocultural criteria which could have incidence upon territorial stability," suggests a minimal area.

> The schema would consist in granting the respective Indian groups full ownership of all the presently occupied and cultivated land plus an extension eight times greater (compared to the cultivated surface) of unoccupied land at the moment of setting land boundaries. This extension of land would not necessarily comprise a single, continuous zone. (Coppens 1971a)

Coppens estimates that rotation in such an extension of land would permit "fauna and flora replenishing" though without giving information as to how fauna replenishes itself. All of which requires an in-depth and perhaps long-range study.

Exploitation of bodies of water. The Guahibos fished in the rivers and streams, and in the summertime gathered turtle eggs on the beaches. In the summer the turtles would come out to the beaches to lay their eggs, and the Guahibo families would go out and sleep on the beaches for recreation, taking advantage of the abundance of food and the good weather. In the winter when the rivers overflowed, it was customary to hunt near the river banks, in the small islands where the animals were surrounded by water.

Fishing in the lakes was primarily done in the summer when it was easier, though it could be done all year long. The fish were more easily seen in shallow water, and bows and arrows could be used in fishing. "Knowing the habits of the fish, their hours of greater activity, the kind of food they eat, etc., makes it easy for the Guahibos to get a better catch" (Reyes and Reyes 1973). Also, when the lakes' outlets dried up one could use the juice of some poisonous plants to stun the fish trapped in the lakes. The same could be done in the streams, using a wooden fence at the narrower end to prevent fish from swimming away.

Fish were never scarce, except perhaps in the smaller streams.

Seasons of the year

From this discussion one can see that the seasons of the year were important to Guahibo economic activity and to the abundance or scarcity of natural food resources. The Guahibos took greater advantage of nature in the summertime, and depended more on their gardens in winter.

Summer (dry season), besides being the work season (land clearing and garden planting), was also the best fishing time. It was the time of turtle and iguana egg gathering and, when sufficient fish was available, for making smoked fish flour for storage. The garden produced sweet potatoes, manioc (year round), and plantains. A variety of wild fruits were also gathered in this season of the year.

In winter (rainy season) the Guahibo depended more on hunting, though it was not very easy due to bad weather. The fruit of the *seje*, *cucurita*, and *moriche* palm trees as well as of the *pendare* and other trees was gathered. The gardens would yield a harvest of corn, sugar cane (year round), and pineapples (in season), in addition to manioc. Mangos and other types of fruit were available in the home gardens.

As was mentioned above, in the summertime the Guahibos would go on more business trips, to attend festivities, to visit relatives, etc.

Tools, instruments, and utensils

Tools used by the Guahibos in their economic activities were mainly for fishing, hunting, and food preparation. They can be divided into things made by men and things made by women.

Objects made by men for personal use. Men would make their own bows and arrows. Bows were made of *macanilla* or *araco* palm wood, and whenever someone wanted a more durable bow, he would use Brazil-wood, although it was not readily available everywhere. Arrows were made of *verada* cane which was specially grown for that purpose; there were kinds of wild cane of an inferior quality. Arrowheads were made of hard wood (preferably Brazil-wood) or of animal bones. More recently metal points have been made. Arrowheads were made in different shapes with specialized points for fishing and hunting turtle, arboreal animals, small or medium-sized land animals, for large animals such as tapir, and for self-defense (Kondo 1973). A few men made blowguns, but their use among Guahibos was not very common.

Men used to make a stick with a very sharp point for breaking ground in planting manioc and corn.

The men made fish traps. When the lakes and streams began to rise due to rain, the men would make the traps to catch the fish as they were swimming upstream. There were two types of traps: *dulíacai* and *yáwito*. The canoe and the raft were used in fishing—both made by men. It is believed that the Guahibos from the Vichada almost never used the canoe in olden times; they made rafts for crossing the rivers. Later they began to make more use of canoes. They had always known of the canoe; it frequently shows up in their mythology.

Objects made by men for women. All woven implements used by women in processing manioc and in food preparation and storage were made by the men of woven strips of a wild cane. The men also wove square baskets for the women to store string-making fiber and other small things. They also made the hardwood pounding mortar used by the women for grinding dry manioc flour, smoked fish, or toasted hot peppers.

The men also wove hammocks and palm leaf mats. They were responsible for building the family house.

Objects made by women. The women made pottery. They made water storage pots, *budares* (the round, shallow plate used for baking cassava bread), cooking pots of various kinds, and several types of serving dishes. All these were made for their own personal use.

The women also spun cotton. The thread was used by the men to tie certain parts of their arrows. Some women used to weave a cotton cloth for the men's loin cloths, but it seems the majority of men and women wore the tree-bark cloth taken from various special trees and made by the women. The women would weave or braid the cotton thread, dyed with various vegetable substances, into cordons and tassels as ornaments for men and women and belts for men. (An elderly lady tells that sometimes men would make belts of their own hair, when men used to let their hair grow and braid it.) Women would make string and rope of palm leaf fiber which men would then use for making hammocks.

Before they had tin sheets which were used to make manioc graters, the women used the thorny roots of the *araco* palm tree.

Musical instruments. Instruments were all made by men and for men's exclusive use. Among them were the bamboo flute, the fox flute, made of a hollow cecropia branch, and the deer skull.

Objects used by the shamans. The shamans made a certain object which they used in the preparation and inhalation of *yopo*—the hardwood saucer in which the powder was made and the inhalator made out of the hollow bones of a bird. The powder was kept in a snail shell or a hollow tiger bone. They also made crowns with parrot or macaw feathers for their own use, a maraca with designs and bird feathers, a collar made out of animal eyeteeth (especially tiger and cayman), and a satchel preferably of tiger hide in which they kept all the implements of their trade to perform their healing acts and other rituals.

Besides the things made by himself the shaman had certain magic substances which he would get by himself or from other shamans.

Things obtained through trading. As can be seen in all that has been said thus far, the Guahibo people got almost all the things they needed from their natural surroundings; for them existence was possible without having to trade for things from the outside. Even so, there was some communication with the outside world, even prior to the arrival of white people into the region.

Certain things were not available in the region. Among them, *palo del Brazil*, a resin used as adhesive, especially in making arrows, fiber of *cumare* palm leaf for hammocks and bowstrings, bamboo for making flutes, and a red dye extracted from certain vine leaves.[5]

Sometimes there was a temporary scarcity of certain products due to crop failure or to some other reason. Then people who had enough of such things to share had a commercial product. This situation happened sometimes with the bamboo for flutes, the hallucinogenic powder, Indian cornseed, hot pepper, and even manioc.

Before white people arrived in Guahibo territory, Venezuelan Indians used to obtain and have ready for trading, first, metal fragments used to produce a spark to start a fire, using the heart of the *fique* tree for kindling, and later on, axes, then glass beads for necklaces. Before metal was available, the Guahibos started a fire by tying two very dry wood sticks tightly together and rubbing a third one between them very fast until a spark was produced. Adults only (men or women) made fire. The Guahibo name for these sticks is *quécoqueco*.

Some Guahibos made blowguns out of a kind of palmwood, but it seems they did not make *curare*; they got it through trade with the Piaroa Indians along the Orinoco and Ventuari rivers in Venezuela. Later on we shall deal with this type of trading in greater detail.

---

[5]Local pigments used by Guahibos to paint their faces were (1) *quérawiri*, extracted by boiling the leaves of a vine *(Arrhabidea chica)*; (2) *cáyali*, mixture of *onoto (Bixa)* seeds, and other substances; and (3) *mapaëto*, made with a tree *(Genipa caruto)* fruit. The first two are red and the third one green, but it turns indelible black (Kondo 1973). The reddish stain of the *arrayán (Myrtus)* tree bark was used to color the inside of gourds and in decorating clay pots. The stain extracted from the *pumaroso (Bellucia sp.)* tree was used in staining arrow ties. In the black stain used in *guapas* designs, *guama* tree sap and charcoal were used. Cotton thread was dyed yellow with stain obtained from some shrub fruits.

3

Agricultural Production and the Division of Labor

The kind of agriculture practiced was one of subsistence. The Guahibo people did not raise crops for the market.

Garden away from the home

Clearing and preparing the land for the family garden was the man's job and took place at the beginning of the summer season (November–December.) At this time the man would go out into the forest to see where to work his garden. After choosing a good plot of land, he would ask his wife to prepare a good amount of cassava bread and other food items and to gather plantains, sweet potatoes, and other vegetables while he did the hunting and fishing to provide the meat. Once everything was ready, he would invite the other men in the village to help him clear the land, and during that day they would eat the food, and whatever was left over, the host would divide among all the workers to take home. This kind of work is called *únuma*.

This is how work rotated every day in the community during the working season; that is, every man would organize his own *únuma* on a different day. The *únuma* is a reciprocal kind of work. After the work for him was done, the *únuma*'s owner owed one day's work to each man who had helped him. If the work was not done in one day, the garden's owner would finish it on his own.

A garden required four working stages: (1) clearing the underbrush, (2) cutting down the trees, (3) burning, and (4) planting. The *únuma* was practiced in each of the four stages except for the third. The first stage consisted of clearing all the underbrush and smaller trees with machetes. In the second, all the large trees were cut down with axes. Some time later, when the trees had been dried by the summer sun, they would be set on fire, but for this work the *únuma* was not necessary, though sometimes it was done by several volunteers. In the fourth stage, the *únuma* would take place for sowing of the prepared land. At this time, it was common for some of the women and children to help.

Bitter manioc, sweet potatoes, plantains, pineapples, sugar cane, and corn were planted in the garden. The largest portion of the garden (about three-fourths) was designated for bitter manioc; the other items were planted along the fringes. Other things planted were some hot peppers and, depending on the person, *capi* (a hallucinogen), fish-poison plants, sweet manioc, cane for arrows, and tobacco.

The harvest of bitter manioc would start nine months or one year later when the tubers were big, though in times of need it could be harvested at six months. Corn would be harvested first after four months; people started to eat corn when it was still young (roasted, in tamales, mush). Dry corn was used to make cassava bread, mush, and other things. Corn, except for next year's seed, was consumed rather quickly. All other crops were also consumed rapidly; they did not last long. Sweet manioc stayed in the ground for one year, but only a few people planted it and only in small quantities, because it was not used to make cassava bread but was only eaten like the sweet potatoes and other similar roots. The bitter manioc was the longest-lasting crop since the tubers could remain under ground from one-and-a-half to two years, depending on the type. After two years they would start to spoil. This kind of manioc was planted every year in order to rotate its harvest.

Once the garden was planted it became the women's responsibility. They would care for and harvest the crops, including the manioc for making the cassava bread. But the garden was considered to be the property of both husband and wife, just like the house.[6]

Home garden

Near the home, the Guahibos used to plant certain things, not in rows, but rather scattered around. Included in this garden, one would find the

---

[6]If a couple was separated, the man would normally keep the house and the woman the garden, but it all depended on the circumstances.

cashew trees, mangos, and papayas. Other things planted around the house as well as in the garden away from the home were pineapples, sweet potatoes, some fruit palm trees, some tobacco, and fish-poison plants. It was also near the house that some cotton plants would be found.

Both gardens (close and away from the home) provided half or more of the necessary food when fishing and hunting were plentiful. Gathering supplied a smaller portion, primarily for varying the diet.

Planting was always done so that some food would be left over, especially bitter manioc, so there would never be a shortage.

4

Distribution of Goods

Generally, the harvested crops were consumed in the same village that produced them. Every family had its own garden and, in addition, gathered wild fruit, hunted, and fished for its own sustenance. The selling of food or paying for services with food was nonexistent; that is, there did not exist a kind of privileged or specialized people who did not plant a garden and hunt like all the others. What did exist was a distribution of goods within the community to establish a balance between those who had and those who did not have on a given day. This distribution was done through sharing. There also was trading of labor and of those things that were not available in all places. All this process was governed by certain social rules and obligations.

Social obligation of helping

The rule was that in order to eat one had to work, and that is why everybody took part in the *únuma*, with a few exceptions. Even the shaman, who was considered a specialist, took part in agriculture and fished and hunted like any other man in the community.

The *únuma* was held for all heavy work, including house construction and carrying leaves for the thatched roofs. Not participating in the *únuma* was frowned upon, and everybody, even those who did not have their own garden, participated. If a man had a wound that did not allow him to take part in the *únuma*, he could later help the person to whom he owed one day's work; he always remembered that he owed that debt.

29

If a man was sick for a long time, the other men did an *únuma* for him, and he would be indebted, having to work for each one of them later when he felt better. If he was an old man, unable to work and without any sons or sons-in-law, sometimes the community leader would invite the rest of the men to do an *únuma* for him, free of charge. The elderly man's wife would provide the food, using produce from her own garden.

Widows did not have anybody to work for them in their gardens, but their brothers would give them a manioc patch for their own use. Or if they had a ten- to twelve-year-old boy, they would send him to work in the *únuma,* even though he could not do much, and then the men would help him in his own *únuma,* because neither the work hours nor the effort was ever kept track of. One day's work was paid for with another work day, regardless of whether one day was longer than the other, according to the size of the garden or the number of workers. What mattered was to be united. When an older man could not work as hard as a younger one, they would reason this way, "But in his good days he did work." They knew that in the end all things came out even.

Social obligation of sharing

When a widow had no close relatives, all the people in the community supported her. The widow would use the *waquena* system, which consisted of herself or a small son showing up at another woman's garden to be given some manioc or where meat was being distributed to get her/his portion.

A good Guahibo man or woman had to share part of his/her own food, not just with widows but also with other people. For instance, if a woman made cassava bread and it was not too little, she would give each of the other families their portion of cassava bread. By giving cassava bread to her own relatives she was showing that she held them in esteem, and so she had to share with them even when they already had their own cassava bread. This sharing was a part of her own personal effort.

The same applied to game brought home by the man of the house. Since it is the woman who prepares the food, it is she who distributes the game meat. She would give each one his/her own portion. If the catch was large, a deer for instance, the man would cut up the meat into pieces, and then the woman would distribute the portions. It was a social norm to give all other people their part. Whoever did not do so was stingy (*asiwa*) and frowned upon by society. In addition to sharing the meat, they would prepare a broth and invite all the men to enjoy it.

A relative, living at some distance and hearing that a relative of his had brought some game, would calculate if some meat would still be left after all other families living nearby had received their portion, and if it was a large animal, or many animals, or a lot of fish, this person would go to the place where the game or the fish was, knowing that he/she, too, would be given a portion. Showing up to claim one's own part was a norm in the society, the same as sharing the product of everyone's efforts among all the people in the community.

If the catch was not enough to distribute among all the people, sometimes the family would make soup and send a bowlful of it to each family, as far as it would go. If there was more, a piece of meat would be given to each closer relative. If there was just too little (less than one pound), they would eat it just in the family, when no one else was around, because they would be ashamed to eat while others had no meat to eat. About game sharing, Lucena (1970–71) writes:

> The hunter ordered the animal to be cut up into pieces, and sent his children, taking different parts of the deer, into the neighboring homes. Entering the friends' home, the child would explain that his dad had gone hunting and he was sending them a little something for them to savor it. It was at that moment that the neighbors felt informed about the event, and even asked kind questions regarding where the hunting took place, etc. This exchange made me think that a hunter's prestige resided not in the individual act of hunting, but rather in the social act of sharing the game with all his neighbors; had he not sent his children out with the various pieces, nobody would have "socially" known that he had gotten any game.[7]

The Guahibos have suffered times of economic crisis when they had to endure hunger (janibo). This would happen when some families did not plant their own gardens due to circumstances beyond their control (epidemics, periods of violence, etc.) or because the crops were attacked by certain plagues and destroyed throughout the community. Whenever such crises happened, the towns left without food would seek the help of those that had it, and those who had food would feel their obligation to help the needy ones to

---

[7]In the author's view, Lucena's interpretation is erroneous, since, as we have seen, sharing was not done for prestige but in order to supply the other people's needs, and because a hunter would have been ashamed to be stingy. It also is an error to mistake the caribi for the dowathi (and to mistake a dowathi for a yajé). Some other interpretations Lucena makes reflect his own way of assigning values without a profound understanding of Guahibo thinking. The reader needs to know that not all written versions by investigators with a short experience among the Guahibos are reliable. Even when an investigator has honest intentions, it is difficult for him to properly interpret the Indians' feelings since a white investigator always sees things from the white man's perspective.

solve their problem since they were their own relatives. Furthermore, they felt the need to be helpful to those who had nothing. Within themselves, they felt responsible and would judge themselves, if they failed to help their fellowmen, since every member in the community knew that he/she was under obligation to share his/her food with those who had none.

When individuals came to ask for food to take to their own communities, they were given a portion of prepared food (cassava bread, for instance) at the home where they asked. Sometimes people would move into another community where there was food, and live there while their own crops were growing. In such cases, generally, the ones with food would give them a section of their manioc garden to feed their families. This donation would be made by the individual who had food for the one not having it. The recipient felt under obligation to pay back the favor in some way, so he would ask how much he owed, but he would often be told that he did not owe anything or that perhaps he could give something of some value (an ax, a machete, etc.) Even when the relative did not demand anything, the beneficiary would always give him something in order not to feel ashamed (*aura*) before his own relative and to not abuse his good will. That is how they would value each other. But when famine would strike the entire area, they had to gather wild fruits while waiting for the new crops to be ready for harvest.

The author will now refer to a specific case that affected him personally in 1981. A group of his own relatives from the Palanas region (Meta) came to the place where he currently lives, Resguardo de Cavasi (Vichada), to live there. The author and other neighboring relatives felt under obligation to help them with food and other home necessities. Since the people came at a time when land preparation for gardens was past, he and his neighbors also had to share their garden plots, so the new arrivals could plant manioc and other things for their own food supply because it is a duty to lend them help according to the customs among all the Guahibo people. Two years after these relatives arrived, all those who helped them received their pay in the same manner.

Here is another example. One year the author and two other members of the community were not able to prepare land for their gardens due to factors beyond their own control. Another community member, who had prepared enough land for his own family garden, seeing they had not done so, decided to give a section of prepared land to each. The recipients were very conscious of the fact that they must respond to him in like manner.

In this case, the author and his two fellow beneficiaries acknowledged the worth of the one who gave them the land to plant their crops; also, the one who gave the prepared land knew that the author and his two companions are worthy, and to demonstrate this fact, he had to share the land he had with them. So, in Guahibo society, no one takes undue advantage of another person's need. To the contrary, in one way or another help is given to the neediest one.

People going as guests to a nearby town did not need to take food for the day. In every village they visited, they were given food—cassava bread, fish, and meat when available. If not, they were given some *yucuta*, and with this food they could feel fine all day. A Guahibo person felt duty-bound to feed any person coming into his home. While working in the gardens it was customary to say, "Let's all work so we can share our food." That is why guests were always fed. Parents always taught their own children this custom of sharing food, even when they were very small.

How tapir meat was shared. The way in which tapir meat was shared and eaten was a bit different. A special feast was organized including various traditional rituals.

Whenever Guahibo hunters would kill a tapir, if they were hunting as a group, they would start dismembering the tapir right where it had fallen, because it was a very heavy animal, and so they would carry it in pieces. If the one killing it was alone, he would have to let the town know so that everybody would come to claim his portion. An experienced man would direct the meat distribution, taking the number of people in the community into account, so as to make an equitable distribution. He was a man who knew the animal's anatomy and the names of its body parts very well. He would give everyone his part. The innards and the hump were equally divided among all the people. Young people were not allowed to eat part of the hump, because it was believed that if they did so they would get old faster. Even the blood was kept, and if they had nowhere to put it, they would stuff the cleaned intestines with it.

Everybody took home his portion in a procession (Indian file), the head up front, then the shoulders and the whole animal would follow in anatomic order. The people would keep shouting, "*Quejeee, quejeee, quejeee!*" so that all those who stayed in town would know that the catch was a tapir.

After bringing the meat home, only the innards were eaten that day. The men would take their respective portion, already cooked, together with some cassava bread, to the house where the tapir's head was taken, to put the food in one place and eat together. Some other food was also prepared.

That night in each home the meat was cooked (smoked) and the next day very early in the morning they would grind it in a mortar. This procedure was performed by everyone who brought some meat. Then everybody would take his own portion of ground meat to the house where the animal's head was being kept and would put a part of the meat in a large, shallow basket from which the adult and young men would eat. The women had another portion in their pots, which they served to all the women, girls and young boys, who would receive it from those serving them in a kind of traditional, almost ritualistic, way of interchange. Everyone, would be given his share, even children not yet able to eat meat (whose share was given to the mother). Expectant mothers would receive two portions (one for the unborn child).

After the meal, they would braid a whip out of palm leaf fiber and blow on it. With it they would give hard lashes at the waist to every willing male, until blood was drawn; sometimes they also struck on the legs and arms. They would tell them that this lashing would prevent what happened to the tapir from happening to them, should they be attacked by an animal or by a person. Sometimes volunteer children would also be lashed with the whip, but not too hard, so they would "become strong men."

They had to save some meat for people from other villages who would come to claim their share. The tapir meat had to be stretched to feed everyone; otherwise, it would be a bad omen since according to a myth, a brother and sister who committed incest were transformed into two tapirs, and as this happened to them, they said that their flesh should go far enough for everyone to eat, and if not, it would be a bad omen.[8]

Eating ground up tapir meat was a social act in which everybody was happy.

The way game was shared. Whenever a large group of people would go out hunting and fishing for several days in a far away place, it was called *camájita*. Some women also went in such groups to help smoke the fish and the meat that were caught. Normally, women with few children would go so the children's crying would not bother the people in the forest. Children would also go along when fishing was to be done in the rivers in summertime.

After several days of hunting and fishing, the group would return to the village, and as a sign that they were on their way back home, they would set fire to the brush alongside the trail. When those who stayed home saw the smoke going up from the fires, they knew that the hunters were on their way back home. If the fires were very close together, they knew that the hunting and fishing had been good. At that time the wives of the men who had gone alone would start to get firewood and water ready.

When the hunters got home, the wives would start to distribute the meat and the fish among those families who did not go hunting. It was customary for each person to take a dish with cooked meat, a portion of cassava bread, and the *yucuta* that served as dessert so that everybody would eat together in one home. The women would share among themselves the same way they did when sharing tapir meat, but not in such a strict ritualistic manner but more informally.

The way things other than game were shared. Upon gathering wild fruit and edible insects, such as leaf-cutter ants, the wife would share her catch with the closest relatives.

If hot pepper or manioc seed was left over, and so it would not go to waste, the wife would invite other women who had less to go to her garden and take their share of it. The man, seeing that a cane for arrows subject to being spoiled if not harvested was to be left over, he would share it with other men who needed it.

As we have seen in the section on common and individual property, the home was shared with those needing lodging. It was also possible to ask to borrow what was personal property.

If a product was scarce, be it hot pepper, cane, or some other thing, there was a way to barter, as we shall see later on.

Sanctions against those not sharing. To understand the Guahibo sanctions against those not keeping the social norms, one must understand the way children were trained at home. Parents were the first to train the children in their infancy. They would teach children their family and social obligations and would chastise them by asking if they were not ashamed that other relatives were watching them. For instance, if the child did not obey

There were two siblings (boy and girl) who did not pay attention to their parents' teachings on the matter of socialization, but rather were always playing by themselves, not minding the rest of the family. Thus, they grew up without knowing to do anything, neither the daily chores nor the social obligations, and without getting to know shame *(aura)*, to the point that all of a sudden they decided to roam through the woods, rivers, and creeks at night. The parents, tired, decided not to feed them so that hunger might bring them back home, but they started stealing food in the gardens that others in the community had planted and were rejected by almost all their relatives, whom they did not let sleep in peace because they ran all over the place, laughing loudly. During that time they also practiced incest. So their own relatives informed *Cuwai* (mythological being with supernatural powers), and he called them in and transformed them into two tapirs for failing to heed their parents' teachings. So they would serve from then on as meat to be eaten by all humanity. So they answered, "And may our flesh be enough for everybody. Whoever does not share our flesh will suffer *bole* (bad fortune). You must share our flesh in equal portions, and whoever is stingy will suffer misfortune. Whoever does not obey his/her parents shall be called tapir so he/she will feel ashamed."

Thus, they gave warning so nobody will commit incest and also established a tradition for when a tapir is killed.

his father's orders to do something, the father would ask him if he was not ashamed to be called lazy. If he did not share his food with his siblings or his friends, his father would ask him if he was not ashamed to be thought of as being stingy. So the Guahibos had this concept of shame deeply instilled in them, and it was up to each individual to give an account for his own family and social obligations so as to not be seen in a bad light and fall into shame. Anyone not changing his behavior (not a common thing) could be directly or indirectly admonished through the words of certain individuals who would remind him of his responsibility. The best person to admonish someone failing to share food or not going out to work on an *únuma* was the male or female cross-cousin. Among more close relatives there was the special kind of respect *(urátane)* that would not allow them to play jokes or pranks on each other, but not so among cross-cousins. Besides that, their parents had taught them to feel shame before their cross-cousins of the opposite sex (a potential spouse), by telling them: "Do you not feel ashamed before your cousin?" So if a man showed himself too be lazy, a girl cousin would call it to his attention; and if a woman did not share the game well, a male cousin would call it to her attention. But to start with, the calling of attention was indirect.

For instance, they would say (in the presence of the offender), "She really gave me a lot of the meat they got, so much so that the food made me sick." Or, "I'm going to be like so and so (gives the person's name) so that others will work for me but not I for them." Or, "The poor thing is sick, but suffers from laziness." They would say these things to shame him/her. Then, if the person did not mind, the admonition could be more direct. For instance (in the case of the lazy one), "Why are you afraid to work? What do you think of a husband like you?"

As we have pointed out before, not keeping the norms was uncommon because everybody tried not to be the one to whom such things should be said, so as not to be ashamed.

But the disabled, the sick, a child, or a widow would be helped without expecting anything in return, because it was obvious that they deserved special consideration since they could do nothing even if they wanted to. That is why no one would ever bother such people, but the lazy and those not sharing food were indeed bothered.

Person's worth determines value of material goods

The Guahibos valued material things according to the degree of familial closeness. For instance, a father fed and clothed his son because he was his son. He did not mind the time or effort it took to do so. He did it because he felt a special kind of love for him for being his son; his son had greater value than the material things he consumed. White people think the same way, but the difference between whites and Guahibos is that the latter felt the same way towards a brother, an uncle, everyone in the family, towards his not-so-close relatives, or even towards strangers because they, too, belong in the human race. So for the Guahibos, the human race is not clearly divided into close family, more distant relatives, friends, and strangers; the Guahibo race is rather an extension of the close family, and the human race is an extension of the Guahibo race. (The word "friend" does not exist in the Guahibo language, because such a concept does not exist; everybody is family.) So not only a son, but all persons are of greater worth than material things.

To white people, material things have value in themselves, unrelated to the worth of the person selling or buying them, or who has them or does not have them. To the Guahibos, material things do not have value apart from the person, that is, without taking into account (as something more important) the person's worth. For instance, if a Guahibo had nothing to eat for whatever reason and if he met another Guahibo who had some food, the one who had food would give it to the one who did not have any even though he might be left without food for the next day (or even for his next meal), without expecting any recompense that would lead to accumulating material things. Guahibos consider people as much more valuable than material things, of greater value than things that could be made, since a human being cannot be manufactured.

That is why a Guahibo thinks of protecting and caring for his children, siblings, and other relatives, as well as those not related to him, because by virtue of being human beings they are worth just as much as any relative. Since almost everybody thinks the same way, they have been able to balance their economy because the beneficiary also values the other person and thinks him worthy of the same or even better recompense. So anyone who is a giver would also be a receiver.

The Guahibos did not take into account the amount nor the quality of things because they knew that whoever gave something gave the best he could give. The latter felt responsible to his fellowmen since he also saw himself as being as valuable as the person receiving something, that is, a person worthy of the responsibility of not taking undue advantage of others.

As a result of this thinking:

1. No one advertised or offered to sell things. A person in need asked. Or whenever someone saw an obvious need, he/she gave to meet such a need.

2. Guahibos did not hold to the idea that the more scarce something was the more it was worth. They did not seek high profits in selling something nor take advantage of a person just because something was hard to get.
3. Guahibos had appreciation for things that were well-made but did not pay less for something not-so-well made. They were ashamed to despise someone's work because all individuals are equally valuable. There were no prizes for doing something well nor for anything else.

Nothing was worth more because it could be given to a certain person (ceremonial value) since everybody was worth the same. It was possible that the shamans' things had somewhat special value, and this fact will be dealt with further on.

Our Guahibo concept that everybody is equally valuable applies to all human beings (Indians and non-Indians) since the Guahibo word *jiwi* means not only Guahibo, but also people in general. When a non-Indian person is visiting, Guahibo folks feel that they must share with him/her just as if he/she were part of the family. But those who understand white culture a bit do not treat them the same way because they know that the white person will not understand. They think that if there is a possibility of offending him/her, it is best not to share.

Value of material goods and services

Among Guahibos, the person needing something (or a service) would figure out the price (or value), not the person selling it. The price reflected appreciation for the salesman rather than the value of the object (or service) in itself. To clarify, let us see some examples.

The Brazil bow. It was very useful in hunting and fishing, and it was not available everywhere. There were times when somebody would come into the home of someone who had a Brazil bow which he himself had made.

The visitor would say to the owner of the bow, "I need a bow just like this one."

The owner of the bow would respond, "If you need it, take it. I can make another one."

Knowing that it took work to make the bow, the visitor would ask, "What do you need as payment for the bow?"

The owner would respond, "Give me whatever you have that would be useful to me and my family."

So the one needing the bow, if he has something that the owner of the bow needs, would give it to him, or else he would tell him, "Go to my house, there I have a hunting dog, a comb, a cooking pot..." or whatever, and when the owner of the bow comes to the other man's home, such things would be given to him.

The owner of the bow would not quote a fixed price for it. The one needing the bow would set the price, but would do so in love. He who had the object wanted to show kindness through it, because he esteemed the person more than he did the thing, and so he did not withhold it from him nor did he put a price on it. And the one needing the object showed his own kindness by paying him with a thing that would be the most useful to him.

On certain occasions, when somebody knew that a relative was in need of a bow, and he had one, he would go and take it as a gift to the family.

Manioc seed for planting. Whenever a relative or any member of the community saw that someone did not have manioc seed for planting his garden due to factors beyond his control, he who had seed would give some to the needy person, even when he himself did not have very much, because the person in need was worth much more than the seed. A Guahibo never charged anyone for seed, because seed by itself, aside from man, was worthless because it was man who was to use the product. This practice was a norm within the society; all the people in the community felt responsible for giving seed to those not having it. If necessary, the community leader himself would tell those who had seed to share it with those who did not have it.

The shaman's services. When a shaman would treat a sick person, be it a family member or not, if the patient got well, the shaman would tell the patient's relative, "He is well now. Nothing will happen to him. Now you must go on a diet and not eat any animal that might not settle well with him. And now I want to ask you to think how much you value that person and how much you are going to pay me for my work. If you do not have much, just give me whatever you can." Then the patient's relative would give him a spear, a bow, some ground hot pepper, a canoe, or whatever he wished to give him. The patient's relative would always give the shaman whatever would be most useful to him to show his gratitude for the favor he had received. They would pay him more if the illness was more serious (if the patient was nearly dying) or if it took much time to get well and took more of the shaman's work.

The shaman almost never would set a fee because he was not too interested in what they would give him for his work. Above all, he was interested in his own prestige, his reputation as a good shaman. He did not think about the things he was going to get, but rather worked just to do good. If he was not this way, he was not a good shaman. (Nowadays, due to the introduction of the white man's economy, the shamans are starting to set prices for treatments in a non-Guahibo style.)

Despite being a specialist, the shaman never took advantage of his specialty to accumulate material things. Also, he was never stingy with his profession; he taught anyone who wanted to learn. But because this process was so long and because of the discipline it demanded, not just anybody could be a shaman.

The shaman's instruments. These instruments had special value among the shamans themselves who knew how to use them. They were instruments used in the preparation and inhalation of the *yopo* powder *(dopa)*, a crown *(sesebai)*, a rattle *(tsitsito)*, and certain objects and substances having supernatural or magic power. The last ones were hard to obtain and perhaps that is why they were worth more than those things the shaman himself could make. But it was the shaman himself who, through his knowledge, made such objects valuable because he was the one who could best understand nature and subdue the environment surrounding the Guahibo people.

Ornaments. In the author's opinion, Guahibos did not have things with other than a utilitarian value. They did not accumulate material goods for luxury, prestige, savings, or other reasons. Guahibos had ways of decorating themselves and objects, but had no ornaments of special value until the arrival of glass bead necklaces, brought from Venezuela after the conquest (see the following section).

A Guahibo man decorated his arrows by weaving designs, with cotton thread made by the women, where the parts were tied together. The thread was then colored with the resin of a special tree *(dacálinae)*.

The Guahibo man would also decorate baskets with designs of varied names, and the women painted designs on their clay pots. They also decorated their tree-bark dresses with vegetable dyes. The shamans decorated their rattles and their crowns with designs and bird-feathers.

Women braided their hair in various forms and wore ornaments such as seed necklaces of various kinds and styles. But the most significant ornament for both men and women was a series of designs painted on their faces.

The paint used in face decoration was *querawiri* or *achiote* and it was applied using a small wooden stick having a small ball on one end. The Guahibos knew various designs which they used to express a person's thoughts. The different designs meant affection, love towards a sweetheart, power, anger, laughter, mockery, etc. So painting one's face was more than simply ornament (see figure 2).

Figure 2. Decorative facial designs

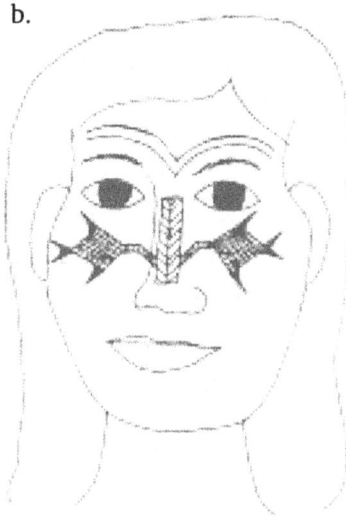

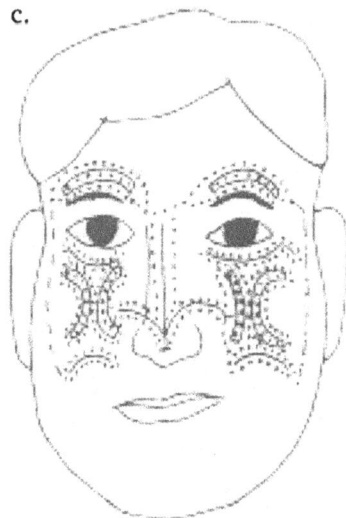

a. *iculijuma-itanexuti* 'design of a tortoise shell'
b. *janeribo-itanexuti* 'design of the pampano fish'
c. a design for men

The exclusively ornamental objects (such as the seed necklaces) were not interchanged and so they lacked intrinsic value. The dyes (utilitarian) were interchanged.

The first things introduced into the culture. Glass bead strands and axes were the first objects to enter the Guahibo economy. These two things came through other Indian groups long before the arrival of white merchants to the Guahibo region. Both objects became priority items for the Guahibos. Axes had utilitarian value since they improved the agricultural technology, and they were included in the trading chain, about which more will be said later on. The bead necklace was the first thing, in this author's opinion, that had more of a social than utilitarian value. The accumulation of bead necklaces (e.g., having many) gave a certain level of prestige. This prestige value was in addition to their value as an ornament very much coveted by women. Glass beads were valuable in trading for dogs and other similar things and were included in the chains of intertribal trade.

Approximate values of certain things, after the introduction of iron and glass beads, were the following: (1) a package of unsalted hot peppers (approximately one pound, or half a kilogram) was traded for a *macanilla* bow or a spear; a larger package (two pounds, or one kilogram), for a Brazil bow, a 1.5- in. wide glass bead bracelet, or enough palm-leaf fiber to make a hammock; (2) a Brazil bow was traded for two glass bead bracelets; (3) a small hammock was traded for one glass bead bracelet; (4) a portion of vegetable adhesive (half a pound) was traded for a spear; (5) a package of dry tobacco leaves (one pound?) was traded for a Brazil bow; and (6) a tapir-hunting dog was traded for two axes and a miner's pick (or a deep frying pan), plus twelve strands of glass bead necklaces, plus a Brazil bow and a spear.

It is possible that glass beads had a more standard price because they came from outside the Guahibo culture and were obtained from the Europeans, who put prices on things. The prices for other things included the worth and effort of the person for making them or traveling to obtain them. Everybody knew the approximate minimum cost of the main items that were traded, but this cost was a secondary value. The person was worth more and if anyone needed something but had no way to pay for it, he/she could get it free.

The way business was conducted

It was primarily the men who conducted business though we have seen that it was a woman's job to distribute the game meat and the agricultural produce, and it was also primarily the women who would show up to claim their share of things *(waquena)*. All other things mentioned in the section on objects obtained through trade, such as Brazil bows, adhesive, dyes, cane for arrows, hot peppers, etc., were traded by the men. Sometimes the men, more inclined to doing business, would take long trips to deal with their customers. At any rate, it was the buyer who asked for things he needed and not the person who had such things who offered them for sale.[9]

Not all men were businessmen; usually it was the older ones and those who liked that kind of work, one or two in each village. A merchant could have more than one person *(wijanë)* with whom he did business.

The most complicated and interesting business transaction (it took longer) was a dog sale.

Hunting dog trading system. Whoever needed a hunting dog would inquire of those who came to visit him if they knew somebody who had a good one for sale. If they told him who had one, he would prepare a trip together with his wife and/or another companion. He did not mind the distance nor the troubles that might come his way; what he needed was a dog. To buy the dog he would take an ax, a miner's pick, and a bow and arrows.

On his arrival at the house of the person who had the dog, he was welcome, regardless of whether he was known or a stranger. (In this case he was not yet a client.) Someone would accompany him and his companions, prepare food for them, and after having eaten, the two men—owner and prospective buyer—would talk business.

The owner of the dog, that is, the host, would inquire about the news of the guest. The guest would tell him about all the happenings in every detail. After chatting about a variety of subjects, the visitor would change the subject and propose buying the dog, saying, "It is known that you have a very good hunting dog, and I do not even have a dog that, though not being a good hunter, could at least be my companion. Although you and I have never done business before, I have brought these things along," and immediately he would bring out the axe, the miner's pick, the bow, and the spear, and would go on. "I know that you need these things and, since I need the dog, that is why I have made this long, difficult trip."

At first the dog's owner, not knowing the other person well, would deny having a hunting dog. He would normally answer, "It is true that when one travels to some place it is because one has a need, and I am very sorry that I

---

[9]A modern instance can be mentioned here about a Guahibo who had a record player given to him in payment of a debt. He was not using it and complained that he did not need it. When asked why he had not sold it, he answered, "Because nobody has told me that he/she needs it."

do not have a dog like the one you need to go hunting and get the meat you need to feed the children in your home, but perhaps you have been told lies. I do not have a hunting dog. I only have a dog that is good for nothing."

The other man would go on to say, "It does not matter if the dog you have is not good for anything. I'll take it. I know you are not going to lie to me because you are a good and honorable person like me. Nor am I in a hurry to go back. I'll be here until I can take the dog." They would carry on like that for hours. If the guest needed to stay one or two nights in the home of the man who owned the dog, he did so. He would stay until he could take the dog. The one who came for the dog used to talk like that, positively. Whenever the dog's owner would say that the dog was not a hunting dog, the one wanting to buy it would say, "It will be good for me. With me it is going to do hunting; it's going to provide meat for my home." If the owner said that the dog was sick, the buyer would say, "That is all right, I'll help it feel better with some medicines I know."

And so they could go on negotiating for hours, until the dog's owner would decide to hand the dog over and to accept whatever the other one had brought as payment for the dog. Sometimes the owner's wife would get tired and tell her husband, "Give it to him."

After that they would remain as clients and every time he needed a hunting dog, he would come to his *wijanë*. They would enter into a situation of feeling mutually responsible for one another. They loved each other like relatives even when they were not. Each one would seek to give the very best to his client.

If either of the two was taking advantage of the other by not giving him the best, the one who felt affected would start to withhold things from the one in need to show him that his product was worth more.

The long chat did not so much mean that one was withholding the dog from the other, but it rather gave him an opportunity to know the buyer well, to ascertain if he was an honorable, trustworthy, and kind person, a person who, in the future, would serve him as client because transacting the sale of a dog was also a way to have some fun for those interested in business. The longer the trip, the better the client, because undertaking the trip was a way of showing appreciation. A traveler, in asking for the dog, would mention the tiredness of his legs so the owner would sell him the dog.

Whenever a Guahibo needed a hunting dog, he would go to a place where somebody had one, taking an ax and perhaps a miner's pick as partial payment for it, and after negotiating and making partial payment for the dog, he would tell his *wijanë* to travel to his (the buyer's) home to receive other things. So the one buying and the one selling the dog would agree on the date on which the latter would travel to get the things offered to him, and then the other would go back home taking the dog he had bought.

When the time agreed upon came, the seller would go to his client's home and the client would welcome him very kindly. Then he would give him a miner's pick or an axe, a comb or a bead necklace, and perhaps a frying pan (or some such combination) so that his client would be content. Sometimes he gave him more than the dog's price and would ask him for another dog.

A dog was appraised according to the kind of game it would catch. When a dog was a tapir or deer (big game) hunter, it was worth more, and so something more like a bow and arrows would be added to the price to make it right. If the dog only caught armadillos, it was worth less. If the dog did not hunt at all, it was almost worthless, but it was not cast out because it always was useful as a companion on the trail, or it would help by eating food leftovers, bones, etc.

If the dog ended up not being a good hunter within eight to twelve months, the buyer could go to the seller and ask for another dog as replacement. Sometimes he would return the first dog, but some other times he would not do so.

Once certain merchandise had been given as payment for a dog, it had to be sold to someone else for the same price, but it was not sold in less than approximately one year, because it had to provide game for its new master for a prudent period of time. Good dogs were in much demand and a good hunting one would change masters frequently. No one bothered to buy a dog that was not a good hunter.

Older people were the ones who would buy and sell dogs; sometimes they were the shamans. A merchant would be accompanied by other people such as brothers, nephews or brothers-in-law, or other merchants. Two or even up to four or five people would travel together. Business trips would always be made on trails connecting one village to another, or on a main trail that did not go by all the villages.

To take the dog home, a special leash (*tramojo*) was used, consisting of a length of string long enough to tie around the dog's neck, a wooden stick about 27.5 in. (70 cm.) long and 3 in. (7.6 cm.) thick, and a longer piece of string at the opposite end of the wooden stick. The stick was used to prevent the dog from chewing up the string and getting loose. The new master would receive the dog tied to the *tramojo*, and the former master would tell him the dog's name. Whenever somebody would travel to another place to buy a dog or to collect a bill, he would always buy other things in the villages along the trail, such as hot peppers, cane, adhesive, etc., because that was his occupation.

When the one selling a dog went to his client's home to collect the things that had been promised to him, he would take a back-pack to carry the objects in. Guahibos seldom traveled in canoes.

The bartering system for things other than dogs. Trips would also be made to buy other things such as ground hot peppers, cane to make arrows, special bows, hammock materials, tobacco, etc. For these things one did not need to have a regular *wijanë*, as was customary for negotiating dogs. These things were often gotten in the nearest villages.

Whoever had no hot peppers would go to someone who had it and tell him that he needed hot peppers to eat with his fish. He would take a bow and arrows to exchange for the hot peppers. They would exchange one thing for another, without taking into account the quantities. Sometimes a small amount of hot peppers would be exchanged for many canes to make arrows.

In the Guahibo way of thinking "many" means more than three, since the Guahibo numeric system counted only up to three, and any number beyond three would be "many." A Guahibo did not need more numbers because he did not exchange a determined number of things. That is, he did not measure the value of an object by a certain number of things, but rather by the effort it took to produce it or the distance one had to travel to get it. So the person's effort received greater consideration in figuring out the price of anything than the number of things; the number could vary.

Business was transacted primarily by the men; the women would just wait for the man to do the bargaining. But exceptions would be made when it was an elderly woman who needed something and she had no husband. She could do business with a woman who had a husband, always with a woman and in the same village, because she could not travel far, being alone. But it was not the norm for a woman to engage in business.

Intertribal and intratribal business relations

There were at least two business chains. One of them ran in an east-west direction; the other ran north-south. It seems that the first one was the more important one as things of greater value or coming from more distant places were bought and sold on that route.

East-west trade. To trade on this route Guahibos from the middle Vichada River would hike from four to eight days, or more, to get good hunting dogs from the Guayabero Indians on the Guaviare River and its tributaries. To buy them, they would take a substantial number of things, such as axes and other steel objects and glass bead necklaces, which they would get from Venezuelan Indians along the Orinoco River. We think that Guahibos living near the Orinoco River got these things from their neighbors, probably the Piaroas. It is known that the Ye'kuana Indians got steel objects from the white people in Angostura (now Ciudad Bolívar) after its foundation in 1764, and later on they got steel objects and glass beads from the Dutch at the mouth of the Esequibo River up until 1814, when the English bought that place and took over trading with the Ye'kuanas. Even later the Ye'kuanas got such things from Pemon middlemen. The Ye'kuana people also traded with the Piaroas, curare specialists (Coppens 1971b). So things passed through many hands before reaching the Guahibos of the middle-Vichada, who would take them to the Guahibos on the Tillabá River in the southwest region of Guahibo land. These folks maintained contact with the Guayaberos and bought dogs from them, and the Guayaberos went to the Guahibos to get steel objects and glass bead necklaces.

It is said that the Guahibos would take dogs to trade with the Piaroas. They probably also took things not available in the Piaroa region, such as bows made of Brazil wood, and things made of cumare palm fiber—hammocks, rope, and fiber from palm leaf for making bowstring and fishing implements. Quite possibly, they also took quérawiri dye for trading, which they kept in decorated cumare nutshells.

Quartz crystals, used by Guahibo shamans, also came from Venezuela. The Guahibos would buy curare from the Piaroas, who specialized in making it.

North-south trade. There also was trading in the north-south direction, which included the Achagua and Sáliba Indians and various subgroups of the Guahibo linguistic family. The Vichada River Guahibos would take hunting dogs and things not available in that region to the Meta River towards the north and trade them for things from that region. Down south one could get adhesives, cumare palm fiber (string, hammocks,) Brazil-wood bows, and a certain kind of gourds. Up north one could get snail shells for preparing the yopo powder, quiripa strands made out of the same kind of shells by the Achagua people (Rivero 1956:6), a kind of stone from the beaches of the Meta River used for smoothing out clay pots, a hard kind of gourd, and possibly axes and glass beads which the Achaguas got through trading with the Carib groups in Venezuela. Hunting dogs were also gotten there, but the best ones were received from the Guayaberos.

According to the Jesuit priests (Gumilla and others) the Guahibo-Chiricoas engaged in slave trading. It is thought that the slave traders were nomadic groups who traveled on the Casanare and Meta rivers and spoke another language of the same linguistic family (Cuibas, Masiguares). Perhaps these were the same ones who traded fruits, meat, and fish for produce with the Achaguas, since they were not agricultural people (Morey and Morey 1975).

Part 2

Interference by a Foreign Economic System

5

Introduction of a Foreign Economic System

In the first part of this book we dealt with the traditional Guahibo economic system. Now we will examine the introduction of elements from a different economic system coming from the outside world. We will attempt to do so in a more or less chronological order, starting by the trade among Indian groups, then moving on to the first white traders and other related topics.

First products of European origin

Traditionally, the Guahibo people balanced their hunting, fishing, and gathering economy with agriculture and self-made things and things traded among themselves and with other Indian tribes. Then foreign articles began to come into the Guahibo economy, things manufactured by white people. As we have pointed out, the introduction of such products was initially done through other tribes with whom the Guahibos maintained trading relationships (Achaguas, Piaroas, etc.). The first articles that came in did not significantly affect the economic and social balance of the Guahibos, but this was the first step towards its disintegration because Guahibos began to "need" foreign-made things. The first non-Indian-made objects that came into the economy were made of steel used for work and glass bead necklaces for ornament.

It is supposed that Guahibos also got certain things through trade with Jesuit missionaries along the Orinoco River, although the subgroups of

51

the Guahibo linguistic family were not limited to the missions (Gumilla 1955:170), and it is possible that the sedentary Guahibos from the Vichada River never lived in such missions.[10]

The influence of the Jesuit missionaries, who worked in the eastern plains from 1625 until they were expelled in 1767, remains to this day in the plants they brought into the "New World." The Guahibos also were recipients of these imports, though in such remote times that they no longer remember when and think that such plants are native to the area. Patiño (1977) points out that toward the end of the sixteenth century the Indians of this region were cultivating plantain, which was brought in by Spanish missionaries. According to Perez Arbeláez (1956) sugar cane and mangoes came in from Asia via Spain (Asia, Malaysia, and the Philippines). The Guahibo names for plantain (*balátuna*) and mango (*maco*) come from Spanish. On the other hand, the name for sugar cane is Indian (*basue*) which could mean that it came to the Guahibos through another Indian group.[11]

Dogs were brought in from Europe, but in the Guahibo region the conquerors found domesticated "mute dogs." Herrera, on a trip up the Orinoco River

[10]Jesuit priests found the conversion of Chiricoa-Guahibos very difficult, as one of them explains it,

> These two nations have been the touchstone of our old and modern missionaries, and the crucible in which their tolerance and suffering were refined; and a field which after having been cultivated through incredible effort and watered with sweat and tears of many workers, has proven barren and ungrateful; and instead of the expected fruit, has produced nothing but thorns and thistles, a generation of gypsies, or a branch of them, who, being given to a life of vagrancy, find any fixed location, though full of greatest comfort, an intolerable jail or an unbearable galley oar. The people of these two nations, who, soon after the missionary priests arrived, reached such heights that nobody doubted their perseverance, but when least expected, they all disappeared like smoke. Finally, in 1725 their conversion was started in earnest; and after five groups were brought into a civilized and rational way of life, having their gardens planted and bearing much fruit, which should have kept them together, suddenly each group went away in different directions and have never again been seen; we were left with the only consolation of the great multitude of children and adults who through holy baptism had gained heaven. (Gumilla 1955:170)

The Achagua nation, perhaps much larger than that of the Guahibo groups at the time of the conquest ("I state that the Achagua nation was extremely large and very numerous" Rivero 1956:59.) was reduced to today's less than 200 people, mainly, perhaps, by the great epidemics which the missions suffered (Morey 1979). Now the Guahibo population is the largest in the eastern plains and one of the largest in Colombia.

[11]"Plantains and yams were the two main species brought in from Africa. Sugar cane, though originally from Asia, came to America from the Canary Islands, the Azores, Madeira, and the African coast, although it was also produced in Spain at the time of the discovery of America" (Patiño 1977:377). Guahibos find it difficult to believe that yams came in from "Africa in Negro boats" (Patiño 1977:373) because they know at least nine varieties of yams, *mapuey* or *tabena*, all with Indian names. The Guahibo generic name is *no*, and the following are some species: *metsajacobejápano*, *pecuaino*, *páwano*, *évino*, etc. On the other hand, the names of many varieties of plantains are Spanish loans, and others are Guahibo.

in 1535, near the Meta River, visited an Indian town where people had *auríes* 'mute dogs' (Morey and Morey 1975). Guahibos have an old myth or story about a family who wanted to domesticate a tiger. It would go hunting for the family, but one day it came home bringing the head of one of the younger children in the family. That tale is why Guahibos think that, except for dogs, no other animal can live together with people. A tiger is always thought of as man's enemy, and a dog as man's friend. This author believes that perhaps in olden times Indians domesticated foxes which are similar to the "indigenous" dogs, they howl instead of barking and are good hunters. "The young in this species can be easily domesticated and they behave very much as common dogs" (Méndez 1970). It is interesting that in the Piaroa language *awari* means fox, according to Vélez and Baumgartner (1962:195).

White merchants

It seems as if the first white merchants (after the expulsion of the Jesuits) who came to the upper and middle-Vichada River regions established themselves in San Pedro de Arimena, in Orocué on the Meta River, and in San Fernando de Atabapo, where the Atabapo River meets the Orinoco River (in Venezuela). The European goods for trading with Indians came from Venezuela by river, on large barges propelled by oars and poles. They were manned by Indian sailors, who also used large hooks. An elderly man remembers that his own father had that kind of work. A crew was from five to eight sailors. Sails were also used to go up the Meta River.

The large, woodburning steamships would bring (up the Orinoco River) dark blue enamel pots, (there were no aluminum pots yet), miner's picks, axes, and machetes from Ciudad Bolívar. They would take cowhides back to Venezuela. At first they had no fabrics. When they first brought fabrics they were of a very poor quality. The author's aunt tells that the fabrics were called *holandilla* (used for lining), *brillantina* (shiny percale used for lining), *tutancán*, and *punzón*. Some of the steamers were named Ciudad Bolívar, El Orinoco, and El Apure.

The Guahibos would travel on foot to Orocué to get machetes, secondhand clothes, and salt (which came in large chunks from the region of the Cusiana and Cravo Sur rivers). They would take hammocks, sieves, *guindos*, *guapas*, *manares*, *cumare* palm fiber, and certain materials used for making brooms.

It is said that in Meta one could get beads for making necklaces, but they were larger than the *mostacilla* which came to the middle Vichada River from the Piaroa Indians. The Guahibo name for the first kind of necklaces was *cuyare* and for the second kind *tulíquisi*. The smaller beads were preferred.

An elderly Guahibo woman, a great-grandmother (one of her great-grandchildren was 16 years old when she died in 1987), used to tell that prior to the arrival of the white people to the middle Vichada River region, her grandfather, who lived in the village of Watulibá, would make trips to Orocué to buy merchandise. Then a man named Jesús (Jesús Churión) came to the village, in a boat, bringing merchandise; the old lady's father agreed to take the payment for it to Orocué (approximately eight days on foot). There the merchant would give him more merchandise to take to his people in the region to again bring him the payment in Indian goods to Orocué.

At that time merchants would come to the Vichada River in their barges, which would go up the Muco River as far up as the Caracarate Creek to get the merchandise coming by river from Orocué to San Pedro de Arimena. The Indian sailors would travel on foot to San Pedro to give notice that the barge had arrived, and the merchandise would then be transported to Caracarate (now Guaramaco) in carts. Then the barges would go down the Muco and Vichada rivers to the Orinoco River on the Venezuelan border. These sailors were those who traded with almost all the Indians along the Muco and Vichada rivers, bringing them merchandise of various kinds, all new to the Guahibos—fabrics, mostly red and of a very poor quality, knives, machetes, axes, fishing hooks, mirrors, combs, needles, thread, matches, ribbons for the hair, etc. They would trade these things for Guahibo goods such as *mañoco*, cassava bread, palm oils, bees' honey, Brazil-wood bows, etc. But the most popular things among the merchants were *mañoco, pendare,* and hammocks.[12]

The author's aunt tells about a merchant, Julio Barrera, who used to bring ponchos, *peleguama araguato* hats, and blankets, among other things. This man was the one who had taken Indians to work at a very good place where they would get much wealth and would leave merchandise with their relatives so they would let them go, but these people never came back. (It is supposed that he took them into the Amazonian jungle to work rubber.) Guahibos trusted him because he spoke their language, but when their relatives did not come

---

[12]Even in the 1940s there still was hammock trading with Venezuela.

At that time there was a very strong trade along the Meta and Orinoco rivers, and in practice national boundaries were nonexistent. The following products were exported from the Vichada region to Venezuela in large quantities: *cumare* hammocks, paying the commissary treasurer five cents per hammock; *balatá* gum and other jungle products were also extracted. All this work meant contracting labor. Up the Meta and Orinoco rivers traveled large steamers such as the "Meta Venezolano" and the "Alliance," which even attempted an invasion of Colombian territory, but was captured by General Buenaventura Bustos, when he was the Vichada's special commissar, without firing a single shot, the only incident of this kind that I know. These ships would go up as far as Orocué which then was a flourishing town. (Efraín Azhavache, personal correspondence)

back, they would ask him about them. He would answer, "There they have everything. For that reason they do not want to come back. They sent you these little things (merchandise he brought). Come on. Let us go see them." That is how he would take along canoe loads of people, and no one ever returned.

Finally, it was the other merchants who started rumors that Julio Barrera's family ate people, and Indians could easily believe it, as, for one thing, he pulled out his false teeth, something Guahibos had never seen before. So all across the region the story was spread that "Damadama (his mother-in-law, Doña Eva) eats people." His wife's name was Narcisa, and he also had a Guahibo woman at the Vichada, whose name was Aleja.

When at last a Guahibo and a white settler (a poor old man) ran away from the jungle with some merchants, they told that no one over there was rich and that Julio Barrera killed anyone who did not obey him. At that time an epidemics hit the lower Vichada region, and many people died. Two or three people were buried in each grave because they could not dig many graves. The merchants blamed Julio Barrera, saying that he started the epidemic. Rumor had it among Guahibos that he had a liquid substance called *amética* which he had thrown up in the air to start the epidemics.

So when Barrera came to Tamaracoco to buy food, the Guahibo people in that village fell upon him, beat him with wooden sticks, and killed him. Pablo Pónare, a Guahibo who traveled with him as a sailor, was waiting for him at the port and managed to escape to tell this story. The best known version of it is Barrera, the rubberman, in Rivera's *La Vorágine*.

Some think that Guahibos did not use *pendare*, but they gathered it to satisfy the white people's needs. The white merchant would set the prices for his merchandise and also for the Guahibo's goods as he saw fit. As was already explained, the Guahibo salesman never put a price on the things he sold.

An elderly Guahibo man from the Muco river remembers when there was only one store in Orocué, and the Guahibos would trade a small hammock for a needle or for a box of matches at that store. Four yards of a low-grade fabric would go for four hammocks. The old man's brother used to tell how in those days a pack of cigarettes would cost twenty-five large, flat cassava breads, three yards of fabric would cost three hammocks, a pair of trousers would cost three hammocks, and a shirt would cost two hammocks.

Toward the end of the nineteenth century rubber exploitation along the Casiquiare River began, and in the Sipapo and Vichada rivers region, the collection of similar products such as *pendare* commenced. During that period, San Fernando de Atabapo (founded by Mr. Solano in 1756) became a center for this kind of trading, and its population grew from about 200 to more than 1,000 just before World War I. Then this kind of trading diminished (Eden

1974). For some time the "dictator of the jungle," Col. Funes, controlled all the rubber and other substances trading in San Fernando and nobody could kick him out, because he also controlled the only access to the region, the passes at the rapids in the Orinoco River. (At last he was brought down by an army led by Emilio Arévalo Cedeño.) Certain merchants from San Fernando traveled on the Vichada River, bringing merchandise to the Guahibos and others, trading it for *pendare*, hammocks, and other Indian products.

Later more merchants came in on their barges with more things to sell. With this competition among white merchants, they themselves motivated the Indians to work more to be able to get more of the things they brought in. Thus, the competition among the merchants lasted a long time and reached the point when some of them said, "These are my Guahibo people, and all they produce is mine." Even though the merchant did not live there, all his debtors lived in that town and that gave him the right to say that they were his Indians.

These first merchants traded with the Guahibos on a system called "advancement," consisting of going into the towns, taking merchandise the people wanted, and leaving some with each individual in exchange for things that they would produce during a period of time set by the merchant when he would return and expect to find everything ready to take with him. Each time the merchant would leave more and more merchandise, setting a new deadline. In that way, the Guahibos always were indebted to the merchant.

White settlers

Eventually, the colonization of Guahibo land started. In order to understand this process of colonization, we shall divide the colonizers or settlers into four groups: (1) the rich colonizer from the plains, (2) the poor colonizer from the plains, (3) the rich colonizer from the interior of the country, and (4) the poor colonizer from the interior of the country.

The rich colonizers from the plains. These settlers were those born in the plains of parents from the same region and who had large herds of cattle. They lived mainly in the Casanare plains, north of the Meta River. The big cattlemen with their large herds had almost no direct contact with the Indians, since they always had a home in a plains town and traveled frequently to various places, but always were present at the "plains work season," the yearly cattle round up when the cattle were branded. The herd administrator (person in charge) was the one who related more to those living around him and did the work or farmed it out to the poor colonizers. At the same time they used to have bullfights and play other games with the penned animals. In this way they could work and have fun at the same time.

The poor colonizers from the plains. They were ones born in the plains of parents from the same region, who spoke Spanish (which included some regionalisms), and whose material wealth was no more than 30 or 40 head of cattle. They lived almost as the Indians did, the only difference being the few head of cattle they had which was the result of his "plains work" with the herds of the rich colonizers from the plains (cattlemen), taming horses, and branding cattle. The poor colonizer always sought the Guahibo peoples' friendship. He never was selfish towards the Indians; on the contrary, he always helped them with his economic resources. For these people it was easy to enter into Guahibo territory because of the services they mutually shared. Sometimes these people would cohabit with Indians by whom they had children. They were called *vegueros* and would plant *topocho* to sell at the cattle ranches. These were the people who began to populate the southern banks of the Meta River in Guahibo territory (now the department of Meta).

But these two kinds of settlers were always different from those from the interior of the country, especially in regards to land holdings, since neither the poor nor the rich ones were people who divided the land because the savannas were always communal property. It was not customary to use barbed wire fences to divide the land, but the owner of every herd recognized his own cattle by the brand and not by the place where they were found. Guahibo thinking was similar, and the Indians did not worry about the presence of white people in the area, because the herds did not hinder their moving in any direction. Besides, usually, if the cattle caused any damage to the Indians' gardens, the cattlemen would pay the damages and lend the Indians wire to fence up the cattle's path.

The rich plainsman owned much cattle in his large herds, but he was never selfish towards the poor people around him. Sometimes he gave cattle to his poor neighbors and almost every week he would give them meat. Because of that, in those times, the rich plainsman had much protection from his own neighbors.

Gold coins were used in business transactions among white people. A steer was worth one *morocota* and there was a saying for those who did not know how to read nor add: *Novillo pa' fuera y morocota la chorota* 'For each steer going out of the corral, a *morocota* had to be put into the box (a calabash bowl)'. The earth served as a bank; those who had gold coins kept them in a clay pitcher buried in a secret place.

The plainsman was used to extending hospitality. He was not selfish; he did not take undue advantage in business; he loved his own folklore; and he sang songs from the plains (*joropos* and their many variations).

Both the rich and the poor plainsmen had similar customs. They both worked the fields barefoot, danced, sang, and played the harp, the *cuatro*, and the rattles. Sometimes the dancing parties in the plains would last two or three days and nights. When they danced, they played stringed instruments and sang songs.

Every plainsman was an early riser. The cowboys went out to *sabanear*, that is, into the savanna to check on the cattle, at 2:00 or 3:00 a.m. The plainsman's diet consisted of beef, rice and, corn, if available, and *topocho*, but especially beef and *topocho*.

The majority of plainsmen were good, but there were also some rich plainsmen who treated the Guahibos badly and would have them killed, and there were also ranch foremen who would pester the Guahibos even though their bosses did not give them orders to do so. The Guahibo people have always been persecuted for owning the plains which are so good for cattle raising. Such is the origin of the term *guahibar*, which means 'to hunt Guahibos', or better yet, 'to kill Guahibos'. As everyone knows, we, the Guahibo people, have been subject to constant persecution from the time of the Spanish conquest to this day. One can cite the example of Planas, in the Department of Meta in 1970 and another well-known one in La Rubiera, in the Arauca Territory, perpetrated on some defenseless Cuiba Indians. But those who did these things were in the minority, and the greater part of the plainsmen living along the river banks sought to befriend the Guahibos.

The rich colonizer from the interior. The wealthy settler from the interior would very seldom establish the farm himself. Almost always he would buy out the poor settlers. Very few lived on their farms; they had men in charge, or foremen. The first thing a settler did upon buying the land was to divide it into large areas and fence it with barbed wire without regard for the resident Indians. Sometimes the Indians were closed in on what he would call "my property." This settler and his foreman never treated the Guahibos well. His purpose was to get the Guahibos fed up so they would move out to a place far from him. Many times this kind of settler would let his cattle (including hogs) loose into the Guahibos' gardens, so that their food supply would run out and they would have to move on to some other place. The Guahibos were constantly threatened by the settler and his foremen who would tell them that if they went on living on "his land," he would have them killed by the police, the army, or other whites. He would accuse them of stealing cattle and hogs. The authorities would always take sides with the rich settler. The Guahibos subjected to such inhumane treatment would look for a more remote place to hide from the evil settler to be able to live in peace together with his own children and other family members, thinking that fleeing was the solution. But this kind of settlement was becoming more and more generalized until it reached today's situation, in which we, the Guahibos, no longer find a place to flee.

The poor colonizer from the interior. These poor settlers started working in agriculture utilizing cheap Guahibo labor, paying them in merchandise, especially poor-quality clothes. This system consisted of the settler bringing merchandise in from the cities and Indians coming to him to get clothing to be paid back in labor. The settler would make everyone a debtor by giving them clothes, matches, fishing hooks, mirrors, salt, soap, combs, and perfumes. Thus, they would be indebted to the settler and ready to work for him any time he needed them. This indebtedness almost always occurred just when they should have been clearing the land for their own gardens. The settler was the one who put prices on the things he traded and would only make accounts in terms of workdays; so a pair of trousers would be worth a certain number of workdays, as would a shirt, etc. By the time an Indian completed the workdays he owed, his clothes were all gone and he had to start owing the settler all over again, taking more merchandise for more workdays.

The settlers from the interior of the country thought differently; consequently, the Guahibos had many unpleasant encounters with this kind of settlers. When the Violence started in Colombia, many peasant families sought refuge in the eastern plains. Once the Violence ended, many families remained in the region. These poor settlers from the interior would come and stay with the Guahibos, and after visiting several places they would strike up friendships with them and pick a spot to establish their *finca* 'farm'. One way to become friends was to be godfathers of the Guahibos. The Guahibos did not oppose such relationships because they never thought that they were losing territory, and they thought the settlers were people who needed to work in order to be able to eat. They never thought of claiming the land as personal property and selling it later on (with additional land) to rich settlers.

These settlers were less considerate towards the Guahibos. Sometimes they mistreated them and called them lazy, brutes, irrational, savages, filthy, dishonest, etc. So there were violent encounters originating on both sides, almost never reaching an understanding among themselves.

The settlers' main crops were rice and corn for selling and plantains for home consumption. From them the Guahibos later learned to plant corn and rice for trading for merchandise brought in by merchants and settlers at harvest time, or given them in advance to get them into debt. So the Guahibos for a long time did not know the worth of their labor or their things, since they were paid for them in merchandise whose prices were set by the settlers or by the merchants.

This encroachment became especially noticeable during and after the period of the Violence. During this period in Colombia, starting in 1948, guerrillas appeared in the eastern plains to confront the government of that period. The whole Guahibo territory served as refuge to the guerrillas and to the large numbers of families coming out from the interior seeking protection in the forests and in the immense plains to hide from their pursuers. Amidst such confusion, the Guahibos suffered persecution under those who took arms; some were killed and others fled to more remote places. Those killing the Guahibos were both the Colombian army and the guerrillas. The army killed them, accusing them of helping to feed the guerrillas, and the guerrillas killed them accusing them of serving the army as guides or informants. The Guahibos were not safe in any case. The best they could do was to avoid both sides and not be in a situation in which either one of them would demand their cooperation.

The Guahibo communities suffered such great violence unleashed by the political forces and greed of that period, which the Guahibos did not understand. They did not know who the conservatives or the liberals were, but they did know that the whites, conservative or liberal, were seeking to exterminate them. (Very little is known in history about the suffering of the defenseless Guahibo people. If anyone were to gather data about these events, it would fill a sizable volume.) Many families vanished that way, and many Indian children who fled their villages died of malnutrition and sickness.

After the period of the Violence, many Guahibos were not able to come back to their own land, especially those who lived in the more accessible regions, because the non-Indian families from the interior of the country who had fled during the time of violence had taken over their land. So they could no longer return and had to stay away in some more remote places, close to other Guahibo groups in order to live in peace. But even this isolation did not help them because the settlers always kept moving out into Guahibo territory. In a sense, the violence has not ended for us, the Guahibos. It can be said that following the period of the Violence, penetration into Guahibo territory by settlers has been accelerated daily, because the settlers remain oblivious to the harm done to

Guahibo communities—taking away our land, the main factor in the socioeconomic development of any people. Ever-improving communications make penetration by the settlers easier so that in the very near future the Guahibo people will be left without even a piece of land for their survival, even though once upon a time we owned almost all the eastern plains of Colombia. It seems as though the Colombian society wants to keep the defenseless Guahibos under its thumb, condemned to disappear, along with our culture, from our traditional land.

Working to get new things

When the Guahibos started having more permanent contact with the settlers, the merchants, and other members of the white society, they saw more goods that the latter had—products of white industry—and wanted to get such products for their families. Some of these things were muzzle-loading shotguns, cooking pots, dishes, cups, kerosene lamps, fabrics for clothes, and mosquito nets. Later on they started to think that other things were also necessary: flashlights for night hunting, shotguns, watches, recorders, radios, bicycles, and outboard motors.

Guahibos did not know how much these things were worth, and when a white person asked a very high price for them, they thought that they really were worth that much. Neither did they know how much their labor was worth. So there were some whites who, without any regard for the Indians, would assign very low wages to the Indians and at the same time put extremely high prices to their own goods so that the Guahibo would always be overcharged and have to go on working to pay his debt. Guahibos knew nothing about working hours, holidays, overtime, severance pay, etc. and nobody wanted to teach them about such things.

The Guahibos were also confused about the way of feeding the workmen. In the *únuma*, the owner of the garden always fed his workers and their families. Whenever an Indian would go out to work for settlers living far from the Guahibo villages, the settlers fed them; but if they lived near the settlers, they were obligated to feed themselves. They were told to bring fish and other things for their food. A Guahibo never thought this arrangement was proper.

New crops

As mentioned earlier, Indians learned from the poor settlers to grow rice and corn to trade with the settler or a merchant to meet his family's needs for goods, something he never satisfactorily achieved. On the Vichada this practice started after the period of the Violence. An Indian would plant an average of two hectares of rice and corn per family. The two hectares would yield three tons of rice and corn combined, which he would turn over to the white merchant or settler who had given him some merchandise in advance. He would then take a few other things and thus remain indebted to the white person. He was expected to pay with his next harvest, because the one who kept count of the price of the merchandise and of the produce was always the white man. So even though a Guahibo was not satisfied with the sale of his produce, he had no other alternative. He had no one else with whom he could trade. He did not know the merchants in the cities, and besides that, he did not know the way of transacting business in the cities. It was impossible for him to travel taking his produce to Puerto López or to Villavicencio, where the settlers and merchants used to take the Indian products to the market. One of the hindrances was that he did not speak Spanish well; he was always despised; his customs were different; and so he did not know how to behave himself. He did not know the market system; he had no vehicle to carry his products; he did not know the value of money well; and he did not know the city address system to orient himself. All these thing made it impossible for a Guahibo to trade outside his own region. Since the settler or the merchant knew that Guahibos had all these obstacles to trading with anyone other than themselves, some merchants and settlers took undue advantage of the situation to their own personal gain and greed.

But as new settlers and merchants gradually entered the Guahibo area, competition among themselves increased, which favored the Guahibos some, but still all merchants and settlers tried to pay the Indians in merchandise rather than money. When they did not have the desired merchandise, the Guahibos had to take whatever was available.

Arrival of money

Since the first white merchants ever to come to do business with the Guahibos used to trade objects rather than money, the Guahibos did not know the value of money. But bit by bit young Guahibos going out to work for settlers in more distant places began to become familiar with money. At first, the Guahibos did not understand why a piece of paper should have value, nor did they recognize the differences between bills of different denominations. When they began to understand the value of money, they saw the need to learn to read numbers, although many of them learned to recognize the bills by their color or their appearance without being able to read numbers. Sometimes they accumulated many coins because, even though they could recognize the paper bills, they had not learned to recognize the coins and their respective values.

When more people learned to recognize the value of money, they started to want to be paid in money, but the settlers always preferred to pay them in merchandise because these did not have a fixed value as currency did, and the settlers could hike up their prices to obtain even cheaper labor.

Cattle raising

The Guahibo Indians working for poor cattlemen settlers saw that they sold cattle to supply their own needs, and some thought that it would possibly be good if they also raised some cattle for themselves. They began buying some cows for raising, but in order to buy a cow, a Guahibo had to face the fact that he would have to work a long time before he could afford it. That is why not everybody could buy cattle. Some were able to get more than others.

They did not know how to take care of the cattle nor how to make good use of them. Some did not consume the milk. The cattle wandered freely all over without getting any salt, causing damage in the gardens and homes of the owner's own relatives, and problems resulted from it all.

Cattle raising also brought changes into the Guahibo economy. Even a new class system was being born into the Indian society based on those who had cattle and those who did not, those who had more and those who had less. For those who had cattle it was easy to get money to buy whatever they needed from the white ("civilized") society. At the same time they learned certain things from that society. Whenever they sold a head of cattle, they bought alcoholic beverages. But even worse than that, they began to be more and more individualistic. They became selfish and undervalued their own culture and other human beings because of money.

Guahibo cultural norms run contrary to selfishness and there is yet hope that they will prevail and the Guahibo cattlemen will see the error of their ways. Many times they have killed a cow when their families and the community were hungry. They have also given some heads of cattle to their own relatives who wanted to start a herd. We will deal with the conflicts facing the Guahibos who have succeeded in cattle raising in the section about the different concepts of property in chapter 7.

Reservations

Encroachment by settlers upon Guahibo territory has been such that the Indians no longer find places to flee. Following the formation of the Colombian Agrarian Reform Institute (INCORA) in 1961, the national government began to establish Indian reservations at the request of the Guahibos themselves. But the settlers did not pay any attention to the Indian reservations. Whenever a settler wanted to establish a farm and chase the Indians out, he did not care if the law was not on his side because he saw that the one expected to enforce the law was a member of his own social class. He also knew how national legislation functioned (or if he himself did not know it, some of his relatives would help him), while the Guahibo people did not know the legal process nor did they understand the legal terminology.

The rich cattlemen settlers moved on unhindered, explaining that cattle raising is one of the foundations of the country's economy, and so it is necessary to flood the natural pasturelands in the plains region with cattle, notwithstanding the fact that they are Indian territory. The settlers' argument was that the Guahibos "do not produce anything for the country." (They do not acknowledge the kind of use of natural resources practiced by the Indians.) Due to this way of thinking, the settler's own conscience does not bother him about the harm he may be causing to other human beings like himself.

If an Indian leader begins learning more about the law in order to help his own people, he is persecuted by the settlers. They accuse him of every kind of evil thing because it is not convenient for them that Indians should have a spokesman to defend their rights.

Cooperatives

Every time the Guahibos wanted to organize themselves to become financially independent from the settlers or the merchants, they failed because they could not find anyone who would honestly advise them in their new venture. If a white person did it out of sheer solidarity with them, he immediately began to be pressured by his own society to not continue helping the Indians. To further illustrate the point, I shall comment, without going into any depth, on the foundation of an Indian cooperative.

In the year of 1966, in the Planas region, Department of Meta, the westernmost area of the Guahibo community, some Guahibos (including the author) founded a cooperative by initiative of a former police inspector. The cooperative was named Integral Agricultural Cooperative of Planas, and it started with seventeen members and a limited capital of 900 Colombian pesos. But as the Indians saw the good the cooperative did for its associates, more and more of them became members until there were 800, and they had five million pesos as operating funds, including the price of a truck, a warehouse, a store, and some land plots to promote agriculture, cattle raising, and a variety of projects such as education and health.

Mention should be made here that the cooperative did not only serve its associates, but it also helped other Indians not associated with it, as well as settlers of limited economic means. Through the cooperative, Indians were able to take their produce to market in the cities in their own truck and at the same time buy those things they needed at lower prices. Thus, the intermediary, settler or merchant, was eliminated. This cooperative was very well-known in the business communities in Villavicencio and Puerto López.

But this was not convenient for the settlers and merchants who initiated war to do away with the cooperative and succeeded on the basis of slander and lies. In 1970 a political war against its founder, Mr. Rafael Jaramillo U., and its associates was unleashed, using public resources to the point that entire villages—both associates and nonassociates—fled into the jungle leaving their towns abandoned. The army was incited by settlers and merchants to persecute the Indians, whom they called subversives, when in fact the Indians were only looking for ways to hide from those persecuting them. Those who fell into the hands of their pursuers were either killed mercilessly or treated inhumanely. The author is a personal witness of these things; he too had to flee and was almost shot to death on February 15 and again on June 9, the same day in which they killed Saúl Flores, Indian captain of Guayema in the Maranai rain forest on the banks of Culimáyuva Creek. On that same day, the author's mother, now deceased, and two younger brothers (one 12-years old) were also captured. They were treated inhumanely and taken into adult white men's jails.

During this massive persecution, the Guahibo people went through an unforgettable period in their history, equal to the shock it suffered during the earlier period of the Violence. The most affected Guahibos were those living on the Planas, Tillabá, Guarrojo, and Upper Vichada rivers, but those in other places, such as the Lower Vichada River, also suffered from lack of food because they had to supply the needs of those fleeing. When the Guahibos fled so suddenly with no time to gather their own children, some small children were lost. Others slept alone in the forest until some relative or neighbor found them, including one of the author's sons who was found by a woman after six days and finally, fifteen days later, saw his own father. Some children could not stand the rigors of life in the forest and died of starvation, exhaustion, and disease. The displaced families lost their houses, crops, and whatever cattle they had, and many of them were not able to return to their own villages where they had lived for a long time.

The settlers were the winners in every way—economically, politically, etc. Non-Indian people interested in keeping the Indian population disoriented succeeded in showing themselves to be powerful, disorienting by force almost the entire Guahibo people, instilling into them the idea that cooperatives were "bad," because as a consequence of the persecution, the Planas cooperative failed, and the Guahibos were afraid to work in cooperatives. There was a time, shortly after the Planas incident, when to mention the word "cooperative" to a Guahibo meant to mention sure war.

Even so, there were other people interested in establishing cooperatives to promote the Guahibo economy.[13] One of them was Father Ignacio González, who created some cooperatives under the name of "communal stores" and bought some vehicles with foreign aid. The Catholic missions and some government programs also had similar projects but also had their own problems though not as violent as the Planas case.

Communal enterprises

This communal system used among peasants of limited economic resources is very little known among the Guahibos, but it is found in a few villages. We will explain here a bit of the history of a cattle enterprise, the one in the San Rafael de Planas Reservation.

---

[13]Many people, based on their own political and economic interests, have interpreted the Guahibo system of reciprocal work, únuma, as a type of socialism or cooperativism, when indeed it is not. As we saw in chapter 1, it is a Guahibo system that makes it possible for everybody to have his/her own garden or house, but not to collect all the produce of all the people in one place. The Únuma Organization, which claims to represent all Indians in the eastern plains, is a very small group compared to all of us Guahibos living in the eastern plains of Colombia. Perhaps the organization's Únuma name is not bad, because it is a Guahibo word, but it should be used with its true Guahibo meaning and represent Guahibo ideology, never as a means of manipulating the Guahibo people by non-Indians wishing to promote their own foreign ideologies.

After the persecution of the Guahibos in the Planas region in 1970, the national government granted a loan to the people on this reservation to buy cattle and establish a communal enterprise. The loan was made through INCORA. Arrangements for the loan were made by the Guahibo leader Isaías Gaitán, who at the time was the community captain. Thus, the San Rafael Cattle Enterprise of Planas was established

The main objective was to raise the economic level of those people who took membership in the association. Gaitán directed very well according to his brothers and associates of the enterprise. It was understood that everybody had to work, but also all profits were shared among all of them since there was a budget for all the jobs. After working all together, they distributed the money among all of them more or less in the Guahibo style.

This arrangement went well for some time; all the associates lived well, more or less, even though they had to pay their debts and the interest. The leader's purpose at that time was to be in good relation with the funding entity and to improve the economic level of all the members using both the white and the Guahibo systems. But unfortunately, Isaías Gaitán suffered some kind of brain disease and was unable to continue helping. After several years he died.

The associates of the enterprise, seeing that the leader was sick, decided to appoint a new president and chose one of the members, the best prepared for the job. The designation fell upon a young man. After the young man assumed the position, the members of the enterprise and the former leader's relatives asked the young man to help them take the sick man to a hospital for treatment, but the young man did not listen to the request for help in spite of the fact that support to do this was almost unanimous.

For this and other reasons some associates began withdrawing their membership and bit by bit the founder's original intentions on behalf of the Guahibos of San Rafael de Planas were changed. However, the program was not an altogether negative experience for the Planas people. What we want to point out is that it veered away from Guahibo principles. Perhaps all these things have helped the Guahibos of this region to strengthen their own economy, taking advantage of the financial aid granted by the state. Even though the enterprise had its flaws, it is hoped that in the future it will be an entity supporting the entire Guahibo economic system, without being swallowed up by the white man's economic system.

In chapter 10 we will say more about the Indian enterprises.

Bilingual teachers and health promoters

As Guahibo bilingual teachers and rural health promoters were trained, a new system within the Guahibo economy had its start. These people are paid a salary by the state for their services to the people in education or in health care. Primary school teachers and health promoters cannot live within the traditional economic guidelines because they do not have enough spare time for fishing and hunting, for garden work, or for house construction due to their special jobs. They work every day subject to a schedule they must keep, and during vacation periods they attend training courses. This obligates them to pay other people to work their gardens and to buy the fish and game brought in by other Guahibos. Even though many of them are interested in helping in community works, they cannot participate in activities such as the *únuma* nor help their in-laws—an all-but-obligatory task in Guahibo culture. They are not able to do these things and at the same time meet their obligations to their bosses.

But they are those who, when they get their salaries, have more money than the rest of the community. Seeing this excess, the community is beginning to have bad feelings because they can see that a new system is being initiated for which there is no explanation within the Guahibo culture. They perhaps start thinking (and the author agrees) that there is the possibility for a new kind of person to emerge, one earning a salary. (Those who worked as laborers on the farms did so only for short periods of time and almost always for the purpose of paying debts, not for a salary.)

Having money, a teacher or a promoter finds it easy to become selfish, not possible up until now. Generally, those collecting salaries try to share them with their relatives. For instance, a teacher has bought some cattle for his siblings. He has also given loans to those who asked him, and they almost always pay him back in labor. It is also a means of generating employment for those who have no other means of earning money. Also, when the people need money to buy something for the community, they require of the teachers and promoters to give more than the rest of the people, and they almost always do so. But there is always a risk because if a teacher, a promoter, or an Indian cattleman decides not to use the Guahibo method of sharing, he could be rejected. For that reason it is good to think about how to help the economy to evolve according to the culture in order to prevent the emergence of classes among the Guahibos.

Thus, bit by bit, aspects of a very different economic system were introduced, and they have had consequences not only for the Guahibo economy but also for the culture in general. As we have seen, the economy is very interrelated with the family and individual worth.

6

Three Socioeconomic Systems

Three basic socioeconomic systems will be explained here, because we believe that such knowledge will help especially the Guahibo Indian to better understand the differences between whites and Indians. Knowing these systems will help him analyze his economic situation and identify his true condition. Then he will be able to contribute new and positive ideas on behalf of the Guahibo people, without becoming confused by interests foreign to the Guahibo society. In each of these socioeconomic systems, the way people live affects the way they think, such as is the case in the Guahibo society. The three systems are: (1) hunting and gathering, (2) agricultural peasant, and (3) money-based.

Hunting and gathering society

This society lives on what nature produces; it is a subsistence economy; it gathers wild fruit, hunts, and fishes. This type of society cannot live in large groups, and is generally nomadic because people must move from place to place, depending on the abundance or scarcity of natural resources. Besides that, in gathering the people use the very materials found in the forests or in the savannas. For instance, when Indians collect *moriche* palmnuts, they weave sacks from the leaves of the same palmtree to carry the nuts. They also do so when collecting *seje* palmnuts. The deer hunter knows how to carry the carcass whole. He crosses its legs toward its neck and so carries it easily on his head. He knows each animal's feeding hours and where to find it. When fishing, he knows what time of year fish are abundant in the rivers and when and how to catch them. He is also skilled in running after animals in the forest.

All people in this type of society live on one economic level and think the same way. Although it is not practical to go around in large groups, on occasions large numbers of people gather together in one place to exchange things, but they do so in times of abundance of fruits and/or fish in the area.

A gathering society is nature-oriented. The supplying of their needs is according to what nature produces. Almost everything is practical. Wherever they go, they build their houses with the leaves they find in the forests or in the savannas. They use tree roots and herbs of various kinds for medicine and magic.

For this type of society the economy is good when wild fruits, fish, and animals are abundant.

Agricultural peasant society

The Guahibos have an agricultural society. They plant everything they need for food and some extras for the market. They take their produce to the market in the cities, sell it, and get some cash to buy the things they need, such as tools, clothes, spices, etc.

People in this type of society do not live in large groups though they may sometimes form small towns, but they are always united. They help each other; they loan money and other things interest-free. They sometimes get together for communal work. They are always hospitable. Most of them are known to one another. Crime is infrequent in this type of society.

They sometimes make good money when the harvest is abundant, but they can also live without money for a while. They do not need to buy food; they produce it themselves. A peasant's wish is to always improve his crops so he can improve his economic condition. Sometimes when they do not have work in their own home or when they are in need, they go out to work as laborers in nearby places. The peasant knows how much his produce is worth but does not try to overcharge for it in order to earn more. Land is very important to them.

They buy some medicines in the city but also have others at home, which they call home remedies. They often do not need to buy medicines or go to the clinics. They almost always want to educate their children in the schools. They have a more or less clear division of labor between the women and the men. They think more or less like their fellow peasants and generally marry peasants in their own region.

Money-based society

People who live in the cities can neither practice gardening nor plant crops because they have no space for these things; they have to buy with money all their food and all other necessities for daily living. Money is the main resource for city-dwellers. They cannot live without money. Only with money can they meet their food, clothing, housing, health, and educational needs. So these people find themselves obligated to get money. He who has money lives well and has everything he needs.

These people have their minds fixed on money, the only solution to all their needs. So they are forced into becoming independent. They do not care about the person living next door to them, whether he/she is poor or rich, hungry or not. In this type of society each individual looks after his own good with little concern for his fellowman. They think that their own resources are scarcely sufficient for themselves.

Those who have no money to invest in businesses sell their own workpower, and professionals sell their time and knowledge. Great contrasts are found in the cities. There one finds hungry people with no place to sleep and with many other needs. One also sees people who have many things and all the comforts of life and who save great amounts of money in the banks.

In these societies there are expert people in all kinds of businesses. They buy things at a price. Then they raise the price to sell them at a profit. They live on the profit they make. That is to say, if they buy something for one hundred pesos, they would perhaps try to sell it for 120 pesos or more. They use the 20 pesos to meet their daily needs and the 100 pesos to buy something else to sell. Or, if possible, they only spend ten pesos and use the remaining 110 pesos to buy other things. In that way they increase their possibilities for making more money. It is also necessary to do things in this way in times when things cost more everyday and money is worth less (inflation). The money they have for investments (to buy new things) is called capital. If they have more capital, they can earn more and live better (have more money to spend more).

Some people do business lending money to others and charging interest (a sum or a percentage for the use of the money) and live on the money they earn by giving out loans.

In the city people work with machinery and establish big industries such as factories for textiles, furniture, or fertilizer, in which many people work for the owner (one or several persons). Everything is geared to making money so as to live on money.

In the cities the houses are more closed in and less accessible because not all neighbors are friends. The majority of the people are strangers, and there are those who make a living stealing from others. Often people are killed and robbed of their possessions. In the cities one sees people living more crowded together and always running around. Those who work in factories and offices must be to work right on time and quit at exactly the predetermined hour. Students also must be in their classes right on time, not even a few minutes late. So everybody has a watch and seems to have become an object, unable to start his duties at his own pace. It seems life is only running and running in order to earn more money.

That is why they lose touch with their fellowmen, and so a sense of insecurity is born. Nobody trusts anyone because no one cares what happens to the other person.

These people are more prone to changing their own ideas and are very divided in their ways of thinking. Often self-concern causes them to withdraw more and more from one another.

They live isolated from nature, and in order to have drinking water they must bring it from distant places through pipes. They must pay taxes to support public services such as water and to pay for their administration. Some of such services include the construction and maintenance of streets and highways, police protection, firemen's services, health services, and schools.

Everybody is a specialist. The medical doctor pays a builder to make him a house and a mechanic to fix his car. He himself does not know how to do it. In order to get a job, a person sometimes has to live far away from the family. Sometimes all the children in a family live in different cities only with his/her spouse and their children. It is not always easy to distinguish between men and women's jobs. They can both be teachers, medical doctors, engineers, government employees, etc. If a person in a community has a farm, he/she normally has machines to do the work and employees to watch over the farm. Finally, this money-based society is very different from the other two types of society mentioned above.

Today's Guahibo finds himself between these three systems. He is a gatherer and a hunter because he gathers wild fruits and hunts and fishes, though he does not depend only on these things. He is also an agriculturist because he plants subsistence crops. And more recently he is becoming aware of the existence of money, though he does not know in-depth the problems that money can bring about. Money can cause a mental illness, when a person who has much of it wants to have even more and more. Specialization has also started with the bilingual teachers and the health promoters.

So a Guahibo needs to understand how the three socioeconomic systems function in order to know what is happening to him and be able to choose the best course for his own people.

7

Negative Effects on Guahibo Culture

Before starting this section, the author wishes to make clear again the meaning he wants to give to two terms which have already been used but will be used more frequently from here onward: (1) "traditional economy" refers to the economic system the Guahibos had before the arrival of white merchants and settlers and (2) "white man's (or new) economy" refers to the economy of the white people (non-Indian Colombians).

In preceding pages, in describing the historical process of penetration by the white man's economy into Guahibo society, mention was made of the shock the Guahibo people suffered. This penetration has affected the traditional economic system and has interfered with our own Guahibo social norms since Guahibos become disoriented and lose control of their cultural norms upon coming in contact with a new pattern, not knowing what to do nor where to go.

Business criteria

The white merchant came in with a new concept, selling his goods at a profit and making money. The Guahibos did not understand this practice, so merchants in those times abused them, charging extremely high prices, while the Guahibos did not at first understand what was happening. Since the Guahibo custom was not to set prices on things, the merchants took advantage of this fact and put low prices on Guahibo merchandise. The Guahibos thought their *wijanë* (client) did not wish to take advantage in the transaction because a *wijanë* always had greater appreciation for the person than he did for things, but the white man did not much care for the person *(wijanë)*. What mattered to him was the merchandise and making more money so he could build up treasures for his own good. Since Guahibos never thought of deceiving to make a profit, they did not understand the white man's system.

The Guahibos saw the advantages of the white man's products such as the axe, the machete, the miner's pick, and other tools because with them they could increase their productive force in agriculture and in artistry (although this was not calculated in terms of earnings, but rather in terms of being able to do subsistence work with less effort). So these foreign tools, brought in by white men, were not what harmed the Guahibo culture. What was harmful was the white man's system of transacting business, aimed at making a profit and amassing a fortune for his own personal prosperity.

This system clashed with the Guahibo culture because as we pointed out above, a Guahibo did not amass personal treasures but rather always shared what he had with others in need. He who had more helped him who had less, without a lucrative intent but rather a humanitarian one. To the contrary, a white man sought to advance himself economically for his own personal status, without taking into account that he was surrounded by very needy people who deserved to be helped by their neighbors.

The Guahibo Indian thinks that one should help his neighbor in order to increase the value of people among themselves. Elderly Guahibos counsel their grandchildren telling them, "Never despise your fellowmen because one person alone in the world is worthless, whereas, if we are many, we will be worth much more. But for this system to work out well, we must help one another, without any selfishness because sharing is not bad."

So the commercial system used by white merchants clashed with the traditional Guahibo economy and culture.

Land ownership

The settlers who came to establish themselves in Guahibo territory had the same concept as the merchants. Their only desire was to make money and hoard it for their own personal well-being. For that reason, they began to work the land with a different criterion from that of the Guahibos. While the Guahibos thought that the land was common property, whites considered it private property. Therefore, the settler's concept, as regards land, clashed with the Indian concept.

There was no room within Guahibo thinking for the concept of dividing the land, to then put a price tag on it and perhaps sell it, since the very thought that land would be for sale never crossed a Guahibo's mind. To him a proposal to buy land from him would be as ridiculous as a proposal to buy his own hand. It is like when chief Seathl of the Dwanwish tribe wrote to the president of the United States in 1885, "How could one buy or sell the sky, the warmth of the earth? This idea is strange to us. Till now we are not owners of the air's freshness nor of the water's brightness. How can you buy them from us?" (El Tiempo, Sunday readings, March 3, 1985).[14]

The rich settler divided the land with high, barbed wire fences into large cattle and horse breeding grounds. Such fences impeded the free movement of Guahibos through the land. Prior to the arrival of the settlers, the Guahibos walked freely, hunting in the forests and fishing in the rivers and lakes, and visiting people in other Indian villages because the savannas, forests, creeks, lakes, etc. belonged to everybody, just like the sky, the rain, and the wind. So they could not understand the white people, who forbade fishing in "their" lake and hunting in "their" woods. Here one sees the great shock the Guahibos suffered not being able to hunt nor fish freely in their own territory, or seeing that the settler accused him of stealing cattle as he went through that plot of land over which the settler was now "lord and master."

To a Guahibo, the land has always been the foundation of his traditional economy since he was not a merchant selling it for profit. Nor was he a specialist who sold his knowledge or his hand labor. So as the Guahibo loses more and more of the land, his only economic resource is running out, and he begins to suffer from malnutrition and sicknesses, not to mention psychological suffering.

That is why today's Guahibos have learned to give the land to outsiders reluctantly, because they have come to see that the white man's way of thinking is different and that for a long time the whites have unjustly taken advantage of the hospitality the Guahibos have always extended to them, since after having owned a house and given lodging to a stranger out of sentiments of human solidarity, the same stranger has taken possession of the house and has cast him out. Now rather than the Guahibo granting the white man permission for hunting and fishing in his territory, it is the settler who grants the Guahibo such permission or withholds it from him.

---

[14]There are some Indians who sold their own plots of land, wanting to get some benefit, rather than losing it all (as had happened many times before, because they did not know how to fight when a settler would come to establish himself in their midst), but now the Indians can see that they should not sell their land, but they should rather seek ways to protect it lest they are left without a place to live.

Exploitation of natural resources

A Guahibo has always exploited the natural resources for his own use or that of his family. He always found all he needed for living in his own surroundings. Whenever a resource was depleted, the people had to move on to some other area where new resources were found, giving time for the renewal of resources in the previous location. Their subsistence depended on such resources; life without them was impossible.

The white merchant, on the contrary, exploited the natural resources to make money and buy things made elsewhere. His subsistence did not depend on being able to find some resins, fibers, leaves, etc. for his daily living. It did not matter if, in order for him to become richer, all natural resources were depleted, because he could always look for other sources of wealth, perhaps in some other part of the country.

The merchants exploited the natural resources in Indian territory, such as *pendare*, rubber, *chiquichique*, various bird feathers, and animal hides. For this purpose the merchant would bring merchandise the Indians wanted, to get them into debt and take them to work in the jungle where the aforementioned materials were found, generally within Indian territory.

An Indian did not realize that such materials should belong to the Indians themselves, and so rather than demanding that his property be respected, he contributed to its destruction. For working *pendare*, many Indian captains would be encouraged to become indebted together with all the people in the community and then be taken into the forests to extract *pendare* and turn it over to the white patrons.

The Guahibos' dream was to get clothes, tools, and other products of white industry. They were unaware that they were taking part in the depletion of their own natural resources.

For extracting *chiquichique*, many Guahibos, with their families, were taken to the upper Orinoco and the Atabapo rivers where this kind of palm tree is found. Many Guahibos stayed working there up to five or six years without ever going back home because throughout all that time they could not finish paying their debt which was constantly increased as clothing and food were given to them. Some would flee from the workplace when taken without their families, but when the family was taken along, it was more difficult to run away because women and children could not stand the hardships and privations along the journey.

Many Guahibos also contributed to the extraction of animal hides and bird feathers, perhaps not realizing that such an activity could be counterproductive to their own economic system. The white tiger hunter's method was to kill other animals such as deer, monkey, and wild turkey and use them as bait for the tigers, thus depleting the game that was basic to the Guahibos own subsistence.

Since 1980 the merchants have awakened the Guahibos' desire to work in the extraction *of mimbre (mamiri)* usually found in the rain forests south of the Vichada. Many Guahibos have given themselves to looking for this material to sell it and, thus, meet some of their family needs. But this author considers this practice to be harmful to these communities, because it only temporarily helps them meet their needs. Later on they are short of this slow-growing plant, which is used for making a variety of objects in everyday Guahibo life, such as house and corral construction and basket-weaving.

The same is the case with the extraction of fine lumber. Merchants buy it at very low prices and then sell it at very high prices. The Indians sell it very cheaply and then they do not have enough of it to build their houses and furniture. Or they allow white people to extract the lumber, with the same consequences.

In more recent times people have come into our territory to cultivate *coca* and *marihuana*. Some Guahibos, in their desire to solve their economic problems once and for all, have done as whites working in these things do, not realizing that this buisness is harmful to the community's cultural and social welfare. They do not understand that these drugs create hard-to-control vices. It may be that some young Guahibos have been involved as laborers, helping those who engage in this kind of business, and then seeing the great danger it brings to Guahibo society, have abandoned this practice. If some of them are still working so, it is because they are not yet conscious of the personal and family harm they are causing in their intent to make money and be like the dominant society. They could even get to the point of becoming addicted to their own product.

There also is the problem caused by those looking for Indian land to plant *coca* and *marihuana* because such land is further away from the populated centers and from the authorities. Those Indians who did not demand respect for their own land have allowed the destruction of fertile land so much needed for agriculture.

Work

Guahibos suffer as they work for the settlers whose work methods are not like their own. A Guahibo has always worked in *únuma* without having a person by his side watching to see if he works or not. In *únuma* work, each individual is responsible for work well done and the time it takes. A garden's owner is not a work supervisor but rather works alongside the other men.

But with settlers things are different. A work day must be continuous if one is working by the day. A workman cannot stop to chat with his fellow workers because the patron will shout at him or give him a dirty look. He does not want the workers to waste any time. To the contrary, an *únuma* workday is a chatter and fun day because then most of the community members come together. It is on such a day when, aside from sharing in the work, they also share other kinds of knowledge and each one's life experiences. That means that besides working, one also receives teaching through dialogue among all.

That is why, when a Guahibo Indian works for a white patron, he feels that he is not working freely according to what he learned in life. He feels he carries a weight, that of being subjected to a new set of rules which do not allow him to waste any time because he must produce more. And because of that, Guahibos and white patrons have sometimes clashed because they do not understand each other.

In some places where Guahibos have had more contact with white settlers and have worked more for them, their own *únuma* work system has been affected. Now some of them do not want to take part in *únumas*, and such lack of participation spoils the system for others. This refusal to cooperate starts to bring imbalance within the Guahibo system; a new evolution in work begins to take place, one lacking definite boundaries where people do not know where to go nor what to do.

The fact that *únuma*-style work has diminished means that the Guahibos do not know what they are doing. They think that the solution is found through the white man's method, but they do not have money, and if they did have it, they would not know how to manage it, due to their traditional cultural patterns which still have a hold on them.

Those who still go on working in *únuma* are perhaps those who have had less contact with the new economy and those who to this day have not lost their viewpoint on how to value things and people.

Family responsibilities

Responsibility towards the family (and towards the person, which is of greater worth than material things, time, etc.) is very important to many aspects of Guahibo economy. Only one of such aspects will be dealt with here, and it is the matter of Guahibo women marrying white men.

The white men who cohabit with Guahibo women greatly affect the Guahibo economy and society because they do not stay with the parents-in-law but instead take the women to live far away. These sons-in-law do not work the gardens; neither do they hunt nor fish for their in-laws.

Besides, they do not respect their parents-in-law and their brothers-in-law (*urátane* and *yáiyatane*); they do not socialize with them. They do not share food or work with their in-laws or with the community. On the contrary, a white son-in-law sends his Guahibo father-in-law to work for him and at the same time abuses him whom he should appreciate because he lives with his daughter.

Another situation is the white man who cohabits with a Guahibo woman in order to remain in the Indian community and then, bit by bit takes possession of his in-laws' land. Some have tried to do so in order to remain within an Indian reservation.

After suffering such experiences, now there are many Guahibos who do not want their women to marry whites.

Property

As we have already seen, the Guahibo people had some very clear concepts about personal and communal property, well understood by the entire community. The coming in of things from the other culture, things that did not exist in Guahibo culture, has caused confusion and clashes with our culture. Some examples are cited here.

Cattle. Some Guahibos have started raising cattle to improve their status within the white man's economy, for instance, to buy notebooks, clothes, etc. for their children who now attend school, or to have an outboard motor or a bicycle. These Indians have suffered inner conflict due to the clashes between cattle raising and the traditional economic and social norms of their own community. They can no longer share with their relatives as in the past they shared game, fish, and labor. Such a person now starts thinking in a different way from the ones who still go on living within the traditional economy. Sometimes he starts to value material things in common agreement with the whites but also goes on valuing the traditional economy because he is still a part of it. So this individual constantly experiences inner conflict and does not know which way to go.

For instance, a person butchers a cow with the intention of selling the meat and using the money to buy things for his home. Many people lacking economic resources, especially women, come to such a person to claim their share of meat within the *waquena* system. So the one who owns the beef does not know what to do because he knows that such a claim is well within the Guahibo economy and culture. So he decides to give meat to those who make their presence known because otherwise he is frowned upon by those around him. Because of that, he sometimes can sell only one half of the meat, after having kept some of it for his own family, some for *waquena*, and another portion to sell on credit to the other neighbors. The one who has the meat cannot overlook the needs of those not able to get game which becomes increasingly scarce. The person who butchered the head of cattle to sell the meat feels at once shame and pain if he were to deny help to his own hungry relatives when he is in a position to help them. But when the beef sale does not come out as he hoped in order to meet his own needs, he finds himself trapped between two economic currents and unable to orient himself and to decide which of the two economic systems he should adopt in his life, that of the white man or that of his own society.

There are those who take advantage of the situation, knowing that what they are doing is bad for their own society. For instance, some people have cattle in the same savannas where the whole community lives, and the cattle start to do damage to the houses (looking for salt they need), tearing the walls down. They also hurt the cultivated plants and get into the gardens and do damage to the banana trees, the manioc plants, sugar cane, and others. But the owner of the cattle does not want to pay for such damages caused by his cattle, as it would be a lot, and he chooses not to worry about other people's property in the community. He chooses to think that he is another cattleman just like the white settlers. As we have mentioned, in the plains the cattleman is the authority and he does not bother himself with damages caused by his animals.

Guahibos almost never go to the white authorities because the Guahibo system of punishment is different (through embarrassment, *aura*) from that of the white people. But people who have decided not to assume responsibility for the damages caused by their cattle pretend not to understand the *aura* system, and show themselves, at least outwardly, calm, nothing bothers them. Those Indians who have a very few head of cattle, who have started to take advantage, are those whom the whites have encouraged to be like the white cattlemen; some others simply mimic them. It should be pointed out that the Guahibo "cattlemen" generally have no more than 25 head of cattle. But these people, even though they consider themselves to be wealthier, also feel a strong sense of guilt in their own consciences before their fellow Guahibos, having grown up in a culture whose norms are sharing and caring for one another. A Guahibo cattleman has that conflict because he lacks a definite policy as he tries to operate in two cultures whose values clash.

Raising pigs to sell to white merchants ended up being beneficial to the Guahibos' economy. A hog is not worth as much as a steer, but it reproduces faster. So if several school-age children needed shoes (or some other urgent item), a Guahibo who had a few hogs had the means to buy them.

But in order to raise hogs, a Guahibo, used to living in a village together with the whole group of people, had to build his house away from town so the hogs would not do damage to other people's property. Nowadays this becomes more and more difficult to do as land for the Guahibos gets more and more scarce.

The Guahibo people do not have enough leftovers to feed pigs, so they let them loose in the savannas where they feed on palmtree nuts and other natural things. Whenever they have tried to raise hogs within the village, there were problems because the hogs were constantly doing damage to other people's property and this bothered the entire community.

The bicycle. This commodity has been welcomed by the Guahibo people because of its usefulness in transportation. Since 1980 it has become an almost indispensable item for traveling from village to village because one can get there fast, even when the distances are long.

Since almost everybody in the community wants to travel on a bicycle, those who have them get into all kinds of trouble. For instance, when a Guahibo has a bicycle, the other people want him to lend them his bicycle every time they need to travel to a neighboring village. But the bicycle owner does so very unwillingly because he has learned that the more the bicycle is used the sooner it will start needing new parts. Then the owner has to spend money on new parts since the borrowers do not think about it; they only want to enjoy the service. (A bicycle deteriorates very rapidly in the savannas because the trails are very narrow and full of potholes. After six months a new bicycle starts needing new parts.) A bicycle owner feels ashamed having to deny his neighbors the use of it, since in traditional Guahibo culture to refuse a service while in a position to do so is frowned upon. So he always finds himself obligated to lend the bicycle, even though he can see that later he will have to buy new parts for it.

Buying or selling a bicycle among relatives also causes problems. As we have seen, the system of conducting business was the *wijanë*, that is, trading certain things for a dog (or some other things) and more or less on credit, not so much valuing things but rather the needs of a person. But the one who has a bicycle got it from a white merchant after many days of labor or after having traded a steer or some other valuable thing, so when his *wijanë* comes around, the bicycle owner feels a bit stingy, not knowing how to answer. But as he can see that the other person is in need, he feels obligated to hand the bicycle over to his *wijanë*. In any case he sets a price in order to please his *wijanë*.

In many communities people have tried to rent the bicycles by the hour, but renting did not have any good results. It has rather brought about enmity because not everybody has money to pay such rent. Besides, it is not a Guahibo custom to charge for the use of things. One can take as an example the use of a house. The house belongs to a person, and yet such a person will allow some other family to live in it, but would never think of charging for the use of it.

The bicycle has brought good into the community, but it has also brought different interpretations on the part of those who own bicycles, to the point that some say it is best not to own a bicycle so as not to have quarrels with the rest of the family. Guahibos interpret the matter of services differently from the white people.

So the owner of a bicycle finds himself between two cultural systems, and there is no easy solution to the problem. Those who lend their bicycles might have the hope that later on they also could ask to borrow the bicycle of the person to whom they have loaned theirs, as some form of recompense. Many others also have decided not to lend their bicycles when someone's need does not warrant it; that is, they do not lend them to the young people just for fun.

The outboard motor. The Guahibo who is able to get an outboard motor also meets certain problems. Whenever he is going to travel to a certain place, immediately many people invent a trip to take advantage of the fact that a relative who owns a motor is traveling, to run their own errands. They get on board and if the boat's owner charges them the fare, they think he is a bad person who should not live in the village, not realizing that he who owns the boat and the motor has to buy fuel and oil and incurs other expenses. In Guahibo culture people are used to the idea that if somebody owns a canoe, they can all fill it to capacity without paying anything, and so they expect to do the same when somebody has a boat and a motor. They are not aware of expenses, because they do not know what a white man does to buy fuel, oil, etc.

So certain material things that have come into the Guahibo community, such as an outboard motor, carry the risk of separating the Guahibos farther and farther from one another.

The shotgun. Even though the shotgun is one of the foreign things white men have brought into the Guahibo community, it has been very useful in hunting in recent times and has more easily been adapted to Guahibo culture because, in spite of belonging to one single owner, the game obtained through the use of it is distributed among all members of the community.

Besides, the owner does not normally hesitate to lend it to any member of the community who is going hunting because he knows that if any game is gotten, there will be meat for all the people, including himself. The loan is unconditional as far as the use of shells is concerned, although in practice ordinarily the owner of the shotgun does not provide the shells. But since very often one who does not own a shotgun does not have any shells, the shotgun owner dares not deny him the use of the shotgun for that reason. He always lends the shotgun with the corresponding shells, because he is ashamed to say no, knowing that it all will be for everybody's good.

Besides, a shotgun does not deteriorate as easily as a bicycle or an outboard motor, and the owner of it does not have to worry about the cost of having to repair it because someone else used it.

From all these facts we can see that the Guahibo expects that personal property should be at the service of the community. One can also see that some things have come in which do not fit well into this system and cause conflict both for the owners and for other members of the community.

The school. Another type of property the Guahibos did not have has also come in: communal property which does not belong to nature and requires maintenance. This kind of property includes fences, water wells, etc., but the best known example is the school.

Guahibos had never owned buildings in common; everything has always belonged to an individual or to the family. That is why it has been very difficult for them to understand well their obligation in the construction and maintenance of a school.

People remember the time when a bilingual teacher was appointed to a Guahibo community where there was not a house to be used as the school. He gathered all the parents to build a school. He told them that a house had to be built so the children could be taught there under his direction, and since the building would serve them all, they had to take care of its maintenance. They helped him build the school but never thought about its maintenance. They would always say that it was the teacher's house even though he did not live in it. They helped to build it as they had always helped one another in *únuma*, but nobody helped a Guahibo in the maintenance of his house, which was private property. So they thought the teacher owned the school and even though the parents had helped in its construction and the teacher had explained that it was everybody's house, they never cared if the house was in good shape or not because they did not understand the foreign concept of owning a house in common.

The same thing happens with the foodstuff donated by the Regional Education Fund (FER) to feed school children. The teacher always receives them, so people think they are supplies given to the teacher. Everybody starts asking for his share *(waquena)*, and the teacher almost always has to give it to them, so they will not get angry, because if he does not give those asking their share, they will start saying that he is a good-for-nothing, stingy teacher.

The teacher gets orders from his superiors, telling him that those are provisions for the children. They give him forms to be filled out as he uses the food on a daily basis, so the teacher is subject to two opposite currents which clash. His superiors provide the food for the children, but the rules of his Guahibo culture demand that he who has food should share it with the whole community, and anyone not doing so is accused by his own conscience due to his cultural upbringing.

All of these problems happen because Guahibos and whites do not hold the same concepts regarding property.

Human worth

As we have seen, we Guahibos have an economic system incompatible with the white man's economy because in our traditional economic system we have two ways of establishing values: valuing a human being and valuing material things. But the main thing is the value of a human being. Human beings are worth more than all things. For a Guahibo there is nothing more valuable in this material world than his own fellowmen. In the first place, the right to life must be acknowledged by all human beings. No matter his profession or his knowledge, what one must value is that he has the right to live. And always, in the second place, one values whatever he invents or does. That is why a Guahibo easily hands over to someone else whatever he has made because the human being is more important than the things he makes or has. That is to say, a Guahibo values a human being more than the things his hands have made. Because of that, within the traditional Guahibo economic system, one finds the sharing of food and other goods with other members of the community (not only with one's closest relatives). Among Guahibos, he who does not share is one who does not acknowledge the worth of the other members of the community, and his behavior is not acceptable to society.

So the value of things takes second place. This fact does not mean that things are not appreciated among Guahibos, but that people are more appreciated than things. To the contrary, in the white man's (capitalist) system, things are more appreciated than people. For instance, a white person wants to accumulate more and more money so that he can get more things, not taking into account the needs of other people who might even be hungry. So while Guahibos have the needs of their fellowmen in their hearts, the white man has money in his heart, without concern for the lives of others. The gadgets he invents help him to devalue himself and other people, without attempting to seek the welfare of others.

Guahibos have always suffered psychological shock as they began to know the white man's economic system. It is been hard for them to understand the worth of money since it has a symbolic value of things and not of people. The author well remembers the time when he had started to know the white society's system, more or less. He went to Bogotá, and one day as he was walking along the streets in the northern sector of the city, he saw two policemen mercilessly kicking and beating a 22-year-old woman with a stick. Seeing that, he asked one of his companions why the men were beating the woman, and he responded that it was customary to do so to get unkempt people out of those places. People in dirty clothes were not allowed in those streets. The author found that impossible to believe, but later he realized that such things were common. That could never take place in Guahibo society, because all people are considered to be very valuable and every one of them is equally valuable.

The author, after a long time of comparative research on the Guahibo and white societies, has reached the conclusion that the white man has lost much of his spiritual values and because of that he sees the possession of material goods as the only solution. So he even forgets about his own sense of human worth and especially the worth of his fellowmen. An economic system based on this way of thinking, be it capitalist or Marxist, leads to the destruction of everything. Capitalists, who only think about having things and do not give any attention to the worth of a human being, seek to dominate everybody else in order to make more money. Marxists, in turn, value human beings not as such but rather in terms of what they can do for society or the cause (revolution). When a person becomes useless, they start looking for ways to get rid of him or her. But "useless" people, such as the elderly, the sick, and widows, are not a bother to the Guahibos. They are of equal worth as all other people because for Guahibos the worth of a person consists in respecting him/her just as he/she is, even if a person can no longer work. Perhaps in the past he/she was able to do so, and for that reason (or just for being a human being) one must respect his/her right to live. One must not wish him/her dead in view of the fact that life is the most sacred possession in this universe. The proof of this view lies in the fact that nobody wishes his own death. (So do not wish for any one else what you do not wish for yourself.) White people should look for a kind of education in which love and happiness reign, issuing right from the heart and not just from the lips. That is, love for one's fellowman and the desire to help him. Only in that way peace for humanity will be achieved.

Socioeconomic bases

From the previous sections one can see that Guahibos and whites have different socioeconomic bases. Guahibos have always valued a person above material things and have always shared their goods with those in need. Since almost everybody thought this way, the economic base was kept balanced. Always he who had more gave to him who had nothing, even if the object was personal property, since hunting, fishing, and crop-raising were always individually done. Tools of various kinds were also private property, but anyone could use them with the owner's consent, free of charge.

Figures 3 and 4 illustrate the difference between the white man's and the Guahibos socioeconomic bases.

Figure 3. White man's socioeconomic system—money-based

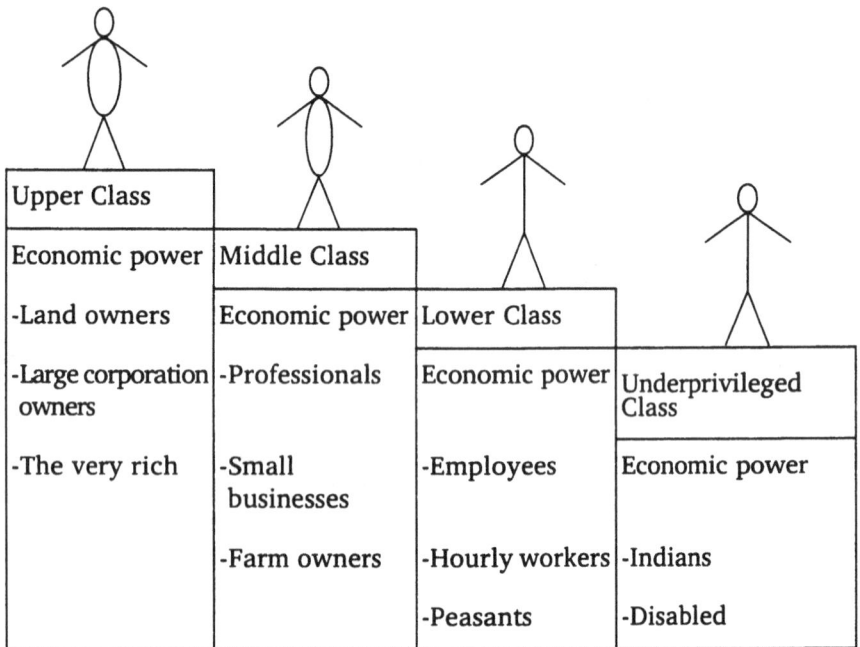

Upper Class			
Economic power	Middle Class		
-Land owners	Economic power	Lower Class	
-Large corporation owners	-Professionals	Economic power	Underprivileged Class
-The very rich	-Small businesses	-Employees	Economic power
	-Farm owners	-Hourly workers	-Indians
		-Peasants	-Disabled

Figure 4. Guahibo socioeconomic system—human relations-based

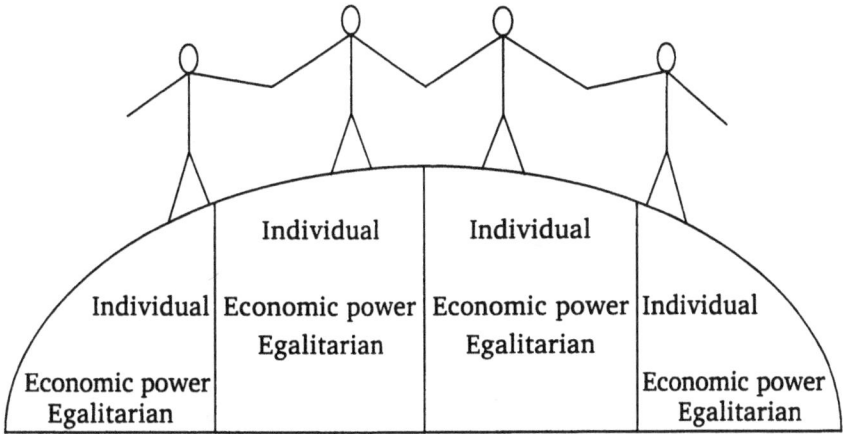

8

Problems and Failures Resulting from not Understanding the White Man's System

In some cases, a Guahibo could understand both economic systems well and still suffer shock, as we have seen in the previous chapter, because each system is different. In other cases, shock results from not understanding the other economic system. A vast majority of Guahibos do not understand the white man's economic system or his form of government.

By not understanding the white man's economy or how he organizes it, Guahibos have clashed with government officials and other people involved in the community's socioeconomic development. Guahibos ask them what they have done with the money that belongs to the Guahibo people, or they say the officials are duty-bound to hand the money over to the Guahibos because they are poor. They do so because when they know that the government or other interested parties have sent some aid to the Guahibos, they think that each of them is personally supposed to get a share of the aid. In other words, they think that those managing the aid are going to distribute it as the Guahibo people always do with game and other things. Guahibos cannot understand that aid designated for the group is not for distribution to individuals. They feel as though they own the aid, without regard for rules and regulations governing its administration. So seeing that the white man does not hand over the money to the Guahibos, they start refusing everything because nothing fits within the Guahibo system.

Neither do they understand the divisions that exist among white people, due to ideological differences, specializations, religious beliefs, social classes, etc. That is why many programs which were started among them have failed.

Capitalist system

As we have repeatedly pointed out, part of the Guahibo problem consists in not understanding the white man's economic system. We will mention some aspects of this system which Guahibos do not understand, due to the fact that equivalents are totally missing within their own socioeconomic system.

Prices. A Guahibo does not know how to do business because he does not know the price of a watch, a ring, a pair of earrings, a radio, a tape recorder, etc. Things in his culture have no price as they do in the white man's culture. He also does not understand the difference in the quality of things and that since some things can be of superior or inferior quality, that quality affects prices. Because of this, Guahibos face many inner conflicts, since they are unable to appraise things according to the need and worth of them to the prospective buyer, or the effort invested in making and transporting them.

There are instances when an Indian buys a watch from a white man and afterwards he realizes that the watch is of an inferior quality, that it is worthless. He finds himself in conflict, not knowing what to do; should he throw it away or try to think as a white merchant does and sell it to someone else who is more ignorant than he about prices of watches. In the long run this practice is bad for those dealing in this way with their brothers. They are frowned upon by other Guahibos who have not yet learned to think like white people do. Within the Guahibo culture a *wijanë* was always offered the very best and if the dog, for instance, was unsatisfactory, the buyer complained. Today Guahibos sometimes complain if the object purchased ends up not being good, if the salesman was a Guahibo. But if the salesman was a white man, nothing can be done. So, not understanding the worth and quality of things can be a problem.

Advertising. A Guahibo never advertises the things he wants to sell since it is up to the person who needs something to find it himself, never thinking that he will be given the worst one. On the other side of the transaction, whoever is looking for something always thinks that he will be given the very best. Guahibos never think that there are people who, in order to sell something, have to shout and say that the object is good when indeed it is not. He is confused by the advertising done by the means of mass communication, such as the radio, magazines, and newspapers. This confusion causes him to become disoriented and insecure as he faces so-called civilized people.

Many Guahibos who have never gone into a city, but like to listen to the radio and understand Spanish, have asked the author if in those white man's houses or stores there are many things likely to be spoiled (as left-over manioc does) because they hear such words as, "We must get rid of this stuff. We're giving things away at incredibly low prices. We're having a sale and so we're selling everything cheap. Come to the great giveaway and pick out whatever you wish." They do not realize that all of these things are only attention-getters to be able to sell more things, good or bad, that what interests them are the sale and the profit. This idea never crosses a Guahibo's mind. He thinks white people are like the Guahibos, that everything they give is good because they value people above things. That is why when they hear these advertisements they want to be present in the store to get their share.

Mission stores. Many Guahibos do not understand why Catholic missions have stores in their boarding schools.

Guahibos generally do not know the purpose of such stores. Some think the store is some kind of a profit-making business which Guahibos think is taking undue advantage of one's fellowmen. There are others who think that such stores are intended to serve the Guahibo people. Others think the stores are Guahibo property, especially when some white people from outside the mission tell them that all those goods in the store are theirs because the government has sent them for that purpose.

Here a Guahibo reaches a point when he does not know what is going on. He experiences an inner conflict and finds it hard to know what is truly real. But at the bottom of it all is the fact that he does not know the workings of the white missionary's economic system. The author believes that the purpose of such stores is to offer parents better socioeconomic help and lighten the burden of the extremely high prices the white merchants always charge Guahibos. But the clashes occur because Guahibos do not understand the white man's system nor does the white missionary bother to learn the Guahibo way to appraise things. And if the missionary does understand it, he realizes that the two systems are incompatible and seeks to impose his own system lest he fail.

Guahibo community stores. Some Guahibo communities have been able to establish small communal stores with the aid of several entities. These stores, in most communities, have had no other effect than to cause discord among members of the same community due to their not understanding the true purpose of the store and not knowing how to do business like the white people do since all of these things are new to them.

The people who provided the funds for the stores seemed to think of helping the communities achieve their own socioeconomic development, but Guahibos have found this method difficult to understand because it clashes with their own traditional system. Guahibos have never had businesses in common even though, due to training and upbringing, Guahibos have always shared things among themselves.

Besides all these things, Guahibos never knew how to figure out transportation costs and include them in the prices. They did not know how to add a markup to be able to make a profit rather than losing more and more each time. They were ashamed to collect debts from close relatives. And so, whenever the merchandise was gone, so was the store. The only stores that have not failed are those in communities where all the people got a good grasp of the system or where there was a good advisor.

Some Guahibos who want to have their own business open up a store with their own resources. But in spite of the fact that the business belongs only to one individual, it also fails because as soon as his relatives see that one member of the family has some merchandise or money, they immediately start taking merchandise on credit or borrowing money from him. As is the custom, the store owner feels obligated to lend money or give things on credit without setting up any deadlines, so he always fails; and if he does not fail, it is because he has decided to think and act like a white man, without any regard for his own relatives, which in the eyes of others is not good.

Sometimes the businessman does not know how much the merchandise is worth and sells things at the same price he paid for them, or even less, if the person asking for it is very needy or is a close relative. If the store does not fail it is because the whole community has accepted the fact that it is as if a white person owned it and because the owner understands the way of conducting business very well. But this could only happen in a community that has had a great deal of social contact with white people and knows their system. There are not many such communities. One way to prevent failure could probably be for the store owner to have enough capital to initially give merchandise on credit to the whole community. Then, after the people are indebted to him, they would not dare ask for more things on credit. And from that time forward he could manage his store like a white man does.

Stores fail due to lack of understanding the capitalistic system and because such a system clashes with the Guahibos' way of sharing.

Loans. Whenever a Guahibo borrowed something such as a bow, a canoe, etc., he knew that he could use the item for a certain period of time. He knew that the object was not his and that he was supposed to return it when he knew that the owner might need it. He would be embarrassed if he did not return it. Likewise, the owner of the object could not apprehend the borrower to make him return the item because he would be embarrassed to tell him that he needed the object, because he could not know if the other person still needed it and that is why he had not returned it.

Because of that, now there is a clash when the Guahibo system is applied to lending money among Guahibos since a Guahibo person is embarrassed to say no or to establish a fixed deadline for one of his fellow tribesmen, knowing that the one asking for a loan needs the money and that it is he who decides when to pay it back. But it so happens that it is hard to get money among us because there are not very many sources of revenue. For that reason, the Guahibo who has gotten some money finds himself caught between two tendencies: that of the traditional economy, which dictates that one should be helpful, and the new system, which says that one should not lend money when it is not going to be a good business deal.

The white man's lending and credit system is even more complex. A Guahibo does not understand what white people do when they lend money with interest. He does not understand that whenever someone lends money with interest, the borrower must return somewhat more than what he borrowed. Guahibos did not do such a thing. Also, he does not understand the deadline arrangement. Whenever a Guahibo loaned anything, it was understood that the borrower would return it as soon as he no longer needed it. That is to say, in the Guahibo way of lending there were no fixed deadlines nor increases to the loan. When a Guahibo bought or sold a dog or something else, he did not raise the price on account of late payment. All that is new and strange to a Guahibo. So when a Guahibo takes a loan from a white man, he thinks that it is the same as if he were dealing with one of his relatives. He does not worry about it because he thinks it is he who sets the deadline for paying back the loan or returning the borrowed object, and he expects to return the same amount in the case of money.

A Guahibo also does not understand discounts in the white man's system (such as in the Agrarian Office) in which a borrower is immediately charged a certain amount for the time he is going to take to pay back the loan. For this reason a borrower does not get the full amount shown in the document. Seeing this difference, a Guahibo many times has doubts, thinking that the clerk had kept the missing amount for himself.

Guahibos do not understand that lending money is a kind of business in which the lender earns more money. And because of that, they do not understand the fact that one asks for a loan to invest the money on something that is going to earn enough of a profit to pay the loan back and still have some money left. A Guahibo will use the money to buy clothes or some other thing subject to deterioration rather than investing it in something that generates an increase such as cattle. The Guahibo economic system did not provide for profit-making, only subsistence, sharing, and caring for one another. The Guahibo system takes care of helping those in need such as the earlier-mentioned case of the widows. So the great majority of Guahibos do not understand the capitalist lending system.

It is helpful to understand both systems: the Guahibo's and the white man's. When a white man talks about economy, he is thinking according to how his system works because he knows it and understands its value. When a Guahibo talks about economy, his perspective is far different from the white man's; the way he perceives, analyzes, and values things is totally different. On many occasions a white man does not find a reason for responding to a Guahibo's complaints, but that is because whites do not know the way Guahibos think, and so whites think that Guahibos are ungrateful and begin forming a bad concept of them. But the same happens to the Guahibos. A Guahibo assumes that whites have understood the way Guahibos think and are now valuing things the way Guahibos do, and so when a white man does not do things the Guahibo way, he is thought of as a bad person. So there are two different systems, and because of that it is advisable, prior to starting a socioeconomic development program among the Guahibos, to take this problem into account.

White man's government

The Guahibo people have never had a central government. Their government is based on local family heads and a network of family ties that covers all of Guahibo land. The people govern themselves according to cultural patterns that need neither a hierarchy nor political divisions. The cultural norms are self-imposed through shame (aura) felt by any Guahibo who does not conform to the rules he learned as a child (Sosa 1983:19, 24–25). For that reason, Guahibos find it difficult to understand how the national government is organized, its hierarchy, its administrative divisions, and its functions.

"**Mr. Government.**" Many times Guahibos think that the government is one gentleman, such as Mr. President, who gives orders to everybody, even to a lower employee. They do not know that the government is upper and lower divisions formed by many people working in different offices all the way down to the lowest levels. There have been times when some Guahibos have gone to Bogotá to have a personal chat with the President, just as they would do with any other Indian captain, to present to him the problems they were having, without regard for how difficult it is to get into his office. (They do not have any idea of what a city is like and suffer trauma when they find themselves in one.) They do not know that the president has ministers and governors with their respective secretaries to solve problems of all kinds and from different regions. They do not know about mayors and policemen. That is why they think that the president is the one who can solve everything. They think that the government is only one person, like one captain in one community but of the white community in this case.

. Many times after the author had gone out to Bogotá to attend to community business, upon his return people would ask him, "What did the president say? What does the president think of us?" etc. They think that when one speaks of the government one is referring to the president, not taking into account the fact that the author barely had contact with people working in sectoral offices and some decentralized institutes in handling Guahibo affairs.

Aid from outside sources. The national government knows almost nothing of the customs within the economic systems in minority groups such as the Guahibos. Likewise the Guahibo people, by and large, do not know the administrative system of the national government nor how it sends the money to pay the number of employees it has. They do not know what parliamentary, departmental, or municipal aid is. All of this structure is ignored by most Guahibos, because they do not know the government and fiscal structures and because Guahibos never had an organization as complex as that of the white man's government.

That is why when a Guahibo leader gets funds or other kinds of aid from the government for the community, other Guahibos do not know how he got the aid and accuse him of having sold community land. And he, being accused, does not know how to defend himself or show them how he obtained the funds, since he himself does not know how the white man's government or his economic system works.

The author believes that recently this feeling of distrust has become more generalized among Guahibos, due to the fact that people from outside the

Guahibo community have taken advantage of the Guahibos' ignorance of the workings of the national government. They feel that people seek to divide them by confusing their captains, so as to use them later to their own advantage, without respect for their Indian cultural principles.

Guahibo leaders find it difficult to request financial aid from government agencies for funding socioeconomic development programs for their own people for the following reasons: (1) because the officials receiving the requests do not know the Indian language; (2) because it is difficult to finance the trip to the cities and offices; (3) because they are not used to, after such a long trip, waiting hours and even days to get into an office to see the person in charge (many times the resources are not sufficient to stay many days in the city); and (4) because the government officials do not understand the way Guahibos appraise things in their economy, and agencies holding the funds do not accept the Guahibos' suggestions because their policies are regulated according to their own interests. Because of all of that a Guahibo sees that there is a big difference between the white man's and his own economic systems; they are incompatible in the way they function and in the way they value things.

Town councils. After the Indian reserves were created, and particularly during President Belisario Betancur's administration, the government began changing the reserves into reservations. Many different entities had become interested in allowing the Guahibos to govern themselves within their own territory through the town councils (*cabildos*) used by Indians in the Andean region, which consist of governors, mayors, and constables. But whereas people coming out from the interior of the country are interested in this structure, Guahibos are more disoriented because they do not understand the meaning of a town council or a governor. Guahibos have always governed themselves through captaincies and understand a captain's role, but do not know the functions of a governor.

For that reason the Guahibos have of late been greatly disoriented by interests foreign to their communities and have come to believe that there are some people who, knowingly and being manipulated by others, want to steer the Guahibo towards their own ideological interest. This is done under the pretext of helping the Indians come out of the miserable condition in which they live.

Guahibos will come to realize bit by bit which system serves them best in governing themselves. Now some communities have even rejected the governorship system. They have decided instead that each town council should consist of several captains, with one of them at the head, under the title of captain general. They opted for not changing the title of captain to that of governor. They have come to understand that in order for a town council to be autonomous and able to function legally, it need not adopt the governorship system.

I will cite the case of Cavasi Creek. When the rumor came that all reserves and reservations had to be directed by governors and not by captains, people began to feel disoriented and the captains felt disenfranchised because they did not understand this policy nor know the labels of reservation, *cabildo*, governor, constable, etc.

They also felt distrust as they, after having carefully analyzed everything, reached the conclusion that those organizations promoting such a change fostered ideological interests foreign to theirs. In view of that, the Cavasi reservation decided to create its own town council according to the people's own interests rather than the interests of those who wanted to organize the reservation for the purpose of claiming that it was *their* own work and that these people were *their* people.

Some communities have adopted the governor system, not because they understand the duties of a governor but only because it was a novelty that perhaps brought some benefit; or at least, they were told that this system would be the best way to relate to the central government and other outside organizations. But the author thinks that this will go out of style and traditional captaincies will be reestablished.

Perhaps the idea of looking for a way in which Guahibos should organize themselves is not altogether bad, but this search should be done for the purpose of helping the community itself and improving its form of government rather than imposing outside systems which cause confusion and chaos. The laws support Indian autonomy, and people seeking to organize the Indians should do the same. They should not take advantage and try to impose their own ideas just because they might have the technique or more advanced knowledge about socioeconomic development. In their own developmental process, the Guahibos themselves must make decisions according to their condition as thinking people who understand their own culture.

It is thought that any entity, group, or person who truly fights to help the underprivileged in Colombian society, such as the Guahibos, must have great respect for their culture and appreciation for individuals as human beings. Besides, every study should start with today's Indians who have to face the modern world and not with the Indians of the past who lived in isolation.

The Cavasi Indians and other groups think that they are the ones who should seek their own orientation. The Guahibo Indian is always ready to know both sides of the situation in order to choose what is good for him, but the multitude of foreign ideologies (of non-Indian society) is still incomprehensible to him and has him always doubtful. Within his Indian culture all people hold to the same norms and think more or less the same way.

It is true that Guahibo society has started to evolve, and in that sense it is appropriate that its government patterns should undergo change, but it is understood that such change should be based on its culture so that the change will not cause interference resulting in disorientation. The Guahibos' system of self-government is important to their social development. Anyone not imposing capricious methods will be contributing to the Guahibos' well-being.

All this discussion does not mean that the Guahibo people are perfect. That is not so. Guahibos are like any other society, with their own positive and negative points. But in these times of evolution, what one ought to seek is to keep whatever is good and discard that which is bad in the Guahibo culture and to adopt what is good and reject that which is bad in the white society.

That is why in recent times the Cavasi reservation leadership and those in other reservations have agreed on having a single policy in resolving their socioeconomic and cultural evolution.

White man's ideological divisions

It is supposed that when a society starts losing or changing its own economic patterns which it had traditionally held unto, it finds it hard to fit into a new pattern. In the Guahibos' case one can see that there are permanent internal and external conflicts. One of the most serious problems for Guahibos who are trying to find their own direction amidst these conflicts is not knowing the diversity of thought found in the white society. They do not understand that among white people there are different ideological currents, and these currents are based on economic power to encourage other people to follow ideological trends in agreement with the whites' interests, even adopting ideas coming from other countries to achieve this economic power.

A Guahibo does not understand that white men do not have a single system of norms as the Guahibos do. He is ignorant of the existence of so many religious creeds (and the divisions within each of them). He does not know the political parties and their internal divisions, nor the various professional specializations with their associations and syndicates. He does not know that there exists a dispute between the capitalist and the Marxist systems. He does not know that when whites fight among themselves and kill one another, it is due many times to ideological differences. A Guahibo once commented, "Whites are very different from Guahibos; perhaps some Guahibo would kill another Guahibo (it is very rare), but nobody would help him."

Because of that, when white people come to the Guahibos, each one talking to them according to his own interests and saying that whatever is his idea is better than what another one has, Guahibos are stuck, not knowing which way to go. They cannot understand; they cannot identify a white man's true way of reasoning.

Part 3

The Direction the Guahibo Community Must Take

9

Developing Understanding

The author thinks that in order for the Guahibo people to be able to function amidst this large number of currents and contradictions confronting them, they must have a clear ideology about a common objective born from the very core of their own society. But in order for such an ideology to be developed, there must be a foundation, and for that the Guahibo society must be educated to seek a common destiny: (1) they ought to be conscious of their own traditional values and the importance of their preservation and (2) they ought to learn as much as possible about the white man's way of thinking in order to be able to evaluate on their own his system and the way it functions. Learning from both currents, we can reach a good conclusion in searching for that which would best serve our fellow Guahibos. Then it will be harder to be carried away by foreign ideologies. Through education we can teach our children the true Guahibo orientation.

At the same time the Guahibo people must show our own cultural values to the white man. Any government program for the Guahibos should be based on a solid understanding of Indian values and customs. Furthermore, the Guahibo people have much to teach whites about human relations and the worth of each human being, values the white man, in his concern and search for riches, has almost entirely lost.

Concientización of the Guahibo people

Education among the Guahibo people should serve in finding a common objective; but to reach such an objective, it is necessary that we learn to

103

appreciate our own culture and learn as much as possible about the white man's culture to be able to interpret and analyze it—*concientización*.

It might be that at the beginning some Guahibo leaders may think it is impossible for us to be educated according our own culture because it would be "inferior to white teaching." But this is not the case. We have advantages; the fact is that each of us from early childhood has received orientation about our values, as also some (many?) of us have experienced disappointments with whites. What Guahibo leaders should seek is to *concientizar* 'raise the level of consciousness of' their people about all the values we possess.

Leaders and people in general should confront the bad propaganda the white ("civilized") people spread about us, saying that our culture is worthless and that the white man's culture is better because it is the one which produces technology for economic development. Guahibos should learn that if we conform only to the whites' economic system, later on we could have social disadvantages as is now the case with the white society which has lost appreciation for its fellowman because it is so taken up with caring for its material goods. This focus on materialism has resulted in abandoned children and terrible vices among those who do not feel they are loved. To get more goods, they engage in the traffic of liquor and drugs, in stealing, kidnapping, and killing. And because they do not appreciate their fellowmen, their disputes explode into civil and international wars.

We Indians should remain firm so as to not be disoriented under the influence of money. The people, guided by their leaders, have to understand that money either causes us to fall into a trap of materialism or strengthens our stability. So we must be very careful as we initiate a kind of socioeconomic development based on a monetary system. If we permit ourselves to be seduced by the love of money, we will fall into error. We will lose our own cultural values. We will become dehumanized because we will lose our love for our fellowmen, and human life will be worthless. Finally, the Guahibos will disappear physically and culturally.

One cannot forget that many things can be done with money in these modern times, but in order to do good, one must know how to manage it. We must not lose the concept that a human being is worth more than money—first, the worth of human life, and second, the value of money and material goods.

That is why it is important to provide true education for the whole Guahibo people so that Guahibos will not go on thinking that it order to be someone in life, one needs to think as white people do. But let it not be an education that only seeks to value that which is Guahibo; no, let it also value whatever is good in the white culture to allow philosophy to develop comparatively, to be able to appreciate what is good in each culture, and to adapt it for development within the Guahibo society.

If Guahibos are not to become disoriented and drown amidst confusion, they must know both socioeconomic systems and which one to apply according to one's need. Guahibos must know exactly the interest or value sought by both the Guahibo and white societies. Thus, they would know what it is that a white merchant (an individual who invests his capital in loans, etc.) seeks. They would know what the white man values most, if it is a human being or the material things he has.

Likewise, the whites would have to know the value a human being has in Guahibo society: that a human being is worth much more than material goods. In other words, what one values is a person's life and not the things he/she has, and that is why everything produced by people should be within everybody's reach so that no one should die of hunger. To achieve this goal, it is necessary to learn not only numbers but also to learn each individual's worth. And they must not just say that people are worth more but demonstrate it through deeds, sharing food, and all other things necessary for life with all other members of the community. Of course, every Guahibo automatically shares because it comes from his way of thinking. It is a conscious duty. Everybody has something within himself which controls him so that each one fulfills his/her obligations towards his/her fellowman, and there is no need to claim one's own rights.

Concientización of the white people

It is necessary to orient all those having an interest in Guahibo problems, especially those involved in government programs, so they will not be ignorant of the true Guahibo cultural values. They must be taught that the way Guahibos see and value things is different from the way white people do, that Guahibos value natural things more than artificial ones. They must be taught that our culture is as valuable as theirs, that it is only different, not inferior.

White people must understand that our kind of education is different, as is our language, but that we think and feel the same as any human being from any other place or society, that the environment in which we live is different, but we want to improve just like any other human being.

We must teach white people to be interested in getting to know the Guahibos better and, thus, be able to help us lovingly and respectfully since it is well known that among whites there are those who care about Indians and are ready to help in whatever way they can.

They should also be taught to be as appreciative of their fellowman as Guahibos are so that they can be properly oriented and able to appreciate the Indian's true value. Teach them that in society human beings are worth very much and that Guahibos have difficulty understanding the white system based on selfishness. So, perhaps, white men would improve the concept they have of Guahibos and know how to help them in accordance with Indian values and customs.

10

Specific Suggestions to the Guahibo People

We have seen that there are different criteria between the socioeconomic systems of the Guahibo and white societies. Now we will try to think of solutions for the Guahibo people in the various aspects of modern economy.[15]

Business

In order to avoid internal and external conflicts, a Guahibo must learn to do business with whites according to white man's criteria. He must know how white people think when conducting a business transaction so that he can make good choices and not feel cheated afterwards. He should be conscious of the fact that doing business with a white person is not the same as doing business with one of his own relatives and that what the white system seeks is to make a profit (that is, the white man's system and not just the behavior of a "bad" white person). At the same time, he must remember and appreciate that the goal of Guahibo merchant's system is to seek ways to help his fellowmen and that goal is something in Guahibo culture worthy of preservation.

A Guahibo must know that the way a white person gives credit is not the same as the Guahibo way. A white person sets deadlines while a

---

[15]The author is open to dialogue with any reader who might have any doubts about the contents of this book or any other related topic.

Guahibo does not. A white man can confiscate and take away things from the one not making payments on time while a Guahibo never does so. A white person can punish the debtor by putting him in jail while the Guahibo punishes psychologically, shaming the debtor. These differences occur because the white man values his things more than the debtor, but the Guahibo believes the other way around.

Whites advertize and offer things for sale, saying that they are of a good quality when sometimes they are not, and that they are a bargain when the salesman is really not losing any money. A Guahibo, on the other hand, neither advertizes nor offers things for sale. A white merchant knows that another white person is going to try to get his merchandise for less money and dicker for a lower price (not to buy it, as the *wijá*.) The salesman then asks a high price so that if he has to come down, he will not lose but would still make a profit. A Guahibo never thinks of hiking his prices or of dickering so that a price will be lowered for him. A Guahibo should know all of this procedure and more so that he will be able to do business without suffering trauma because he did not understand how business with whites is done. But to do business with other Guahibos, he should adhere to Guahibo norms, valuing a person and his needs above material things.

Guahibos must take into account the value of our economic system and not copy the white system, thinking that their system is better. Yes, we have to learn their system in order to use it when dealing with them but not change our system in our own towns.

Land holding

The Guahibo people should be conscious that whites have a different concept from ours in the matter of land ownership. A white man thinks of owning a piece of land for himself; that is, for him, having a plot of land is to have something for his children. Because of this, land has to be partitioned to know whose is the fenced-up plot since having a tract of land is to have a commodity which is negotiable. Whereas Guahibos do not think that way, so Guahibos must not be confused by this perspective. It is good to continue thinking the way they always have—land is for all the Guahibos' benefit. We should not adopt the whites' way of owning land. We already know that it is not good for us. Since some whites do not own land, they do not even have a place to build a house, something so important to everybody's life.

No Guahibo should ever think of selling land as whites do because the new generations would not have a place to live. They should all learn to keep the land for the Guahibo community and not think, as they did before, that whites also had a right to the land, and because of that they were not kept out. Now we see that this course of action has caused great problems to the Guahibo people because whites have a very different way of thinking about property. Guahibos must stop the coming of new white settlers into their own territory to avoid future confrontations between whites and Guahibos.

All whites wanting to come in should be advised not to do so because the land is Guahibo property. And at the same time, the central government should be told to instruct whites to respect the Guahibos' rights to the land that has been theirs from time immemorial. (Invaders who do not obey the Indian captains should be denounced. A complaint is made before the mayor before the invader has been on the spot 30 days, copying other legal authorities, so that records of the complaint will be established.) In reality, Guahibos now have very little land and they have to take maximum advantage of it by making it productive.

Natural resources

Guahibos must understand clearly the white people's motivation in exploiting the natural resources or hiring people to do so. One must know that both Guahibos and whites exploit natural resources, but the whites' interest is different. Guahibos use the resources for their subsistence, no more than is necessary, without abuse, so as not to deplete them, but rather preserving them so they will be available later on. Whites, on the other hand, in their desire to amass wealth, do not care if they are causing destruction since, having money, they can move on to another location where they can continue doing the same; money helps to solve problems easily. Guahibos resolve their problems with the resources that surround them in their immediate geographic and ecological environment.

For this reason, we must not allow natural resources to be abused by whites. Besides, Guahibos ought to hold *concientizción* campaigns among whites and Guahibos, explaining to those making unreasonable use of natural resources that if one thinks of them only as a source of money, not caring about the damage done to them, the land will slowly die. The land has life because plants and animals and water sources are alive, and if these are done away with, the land will also soon die.

In Guahibo territory (eastern plains) one sees how large forests are destroyed by white settlers to plant corn, rice, and eventually pasture grass, and also to establish large sawmills for selling lumber. And of late, since land in tropical forests is not very fertile, they have been using chemical fertilizers which shorten the life of natural resources, so the plains will very soon become a desert. That is why it is the job of all Guahibos and others to advise all those who cause damage that they should not exploit nature with the white people's ideas, but rather allow time for the forest products to replenish themselves without totally destroying them. Using natural resources without exhausting them is to use them sensibly. Everybody should be careful not to destroy them. Many Guahibos should realize that in places where the *morichales* have been depleted they do not have materials to build their own houses.

Since there is not very much land and the population keeps on growing, the author thinks that everybody should continue planting trees as they cut them down; they should plant two or three trees for each one they cut down. They should do the same with palm trees. It is also advisable to plant as many cedar trees as possible as an economic basis for future generations. It is possible that at the beginning this practice might not seem to be valuable, but the day will come when this reforestation policy will be considered valuable. Guahibos, themselves, must seek ways to develop our economy and not be carried away by harmful practices.

Work

It is known to almost all Guahibos who have worked for white patrons that working for whites is not the same as working among Guahibos. Perhaps some who have attempted to imitate the whites are not in good relations with other Guahibos because the results were not what they expected at the beginning. So, the thing for them to do is to continue with the traditional *únuma* so that they will not feel uncomfortable among Guahibos and will not go against the rest of society. The white man's way bothers most Guahibos not used to "not wasting time" chatting with their fellow workers. To avoid this discomfort, we must keep on using the *únuma* whenever we are not working with whites.

In order for our system to work, we should not incur debts with whites, who force us into selling our manpower whenever they please (even during *únuma* time) and at a price set by them. If we do not get into debt, we will be free to work in our own territory according to our traditional system. Then, if we wish, we may work for cash rather than for things as we have free time.

Furthermore, if Guahibos work for themselves on their own projects, it would prove that they are producing something for the nation. When they work for whites, these people say that it is they who are producing, even though those doing the work are Guahibos.

It is also considered necessary to show all the Guahibo youth that it is one's duty to work in order to support oneself and one's family and not allow them to become lazy, as has been the case lately with those who went into the boarding schools to get an education. Upon returning to the village where their parents are, sometimes they do not want to go to work in the fields, nor do they want to learn to weave the utensils for food preparation. We must show them that learning these skills is their duty so that they will be responsible members of the community.

This process should be started as soon as possible so that the young people will not feel disoriented, having already been disoriented by the non-Indian education. In fact, we should demand that even in school young people be taught all their obligations towards society. Likewise, girls who have gone to non-Indian schools should be required to learn all the chores of a Guahibo woman. Girls must take these things into account and not think that they are unnecessary.

Family responsibilities

A Guahibo person should continue fulfilling his/her responsibilities towards his/her relatives, without having to imitate white people. It is clearly seen that Guahibos feel a greater sense of responsibility towards their relatives than whites do. The white system does not have such an effective, psychological mechanism causing people to feel love and responsibility towards all their relatives. That is why one sees abandoned children in the great cities and other forms of abuse against their fellowmen. It is not because white society lacks norms for love and respect but rather because it does not have a great family who sees to it that the values be upheld through shame. White people in large cities do not know their own neighbors. And besides, everybody is very busy seeking a better status and more money. They even fight their own brothers to get a larger share of the inheritance left by their parents.

It is good to make whites understand that our system is good and that that is why there are no killings among Guahibos, while they are common among whites.

It is also thought necessary that every Guahibo father should be thoroughly aware of the problems that could result should one of his daughters cohabit with a white man. A white man should be aware that if he takes a Guahibo woman as a wife, he would not in the least be contributing to strengthening the Guahibo culture or ideology. On the contrary, it will be detrimental. The Guahibo people have already had much experience with parents who allowed their own daughters to marry whites, thinking that they would profit from it, when indeed the opposite happens. The girl cannot live close to her own relatives because her white husband forbids her to do so. In addition, their children are confused because they do not know which one of their parents' families is more important. Many of them are proud to be children of a white man and despise their own Guahibo values.

A Guahibo father must not allow himself to be deceived by the material goods promised to him by a white man for taking one of his daughters because whites often do not respect their Indian in-laws. A Guahibo woman living with a white man will always suffer the pain and anguish of seeing that her husband has no respect for her own parents, and later her children do not respect their grandparents nor their mother's own race. For this reason, it is every parent's obligation to guide his own daughters, so they will not fall into the greatest error and deceit of their lifetime. Life does not consist in having things. Life is having peace and joy within oneself. He who values his own life seeks these things.

Also, in allowing a white man to marry a Guahibo woman one runs the risk that if he does not take the woman away from the family, the white husband starts taking possession of the land, and later on he declares himself to be the owner of it. He begins harming the Guahibo society, showing no respect for it nor being helpful in any way. There even are cases when a white man takes a Guahibo wife only to get the land.

Women ought to think seriously about these things so that they will not be disappointed by the ill-treatment they get. They should know that even though they might live with a white man, they will never be equal to whites, even if they are well educated, since their blood never ceases to be Guahibo blood. They should also remember those who brought them up. Education should help them to uphold their own people rather than becoming dependent on others.

All women who have come to know all the Guahibo social problems should contribute to their solution, and for this reason they should marry Guahibos, so as to not fall into these intercultural problems.

Property

As we have seen, white people's concept of property differs from that of the Guahibos. For instance, if a Guahibo has a canoe, he finds it easy to lend it to anyone who needs it, whereas if a white has a car, it is not easy for him to loan it. A Guahibo's main interest is to serve his fellowmen with whatever he has, while a white man has property in order to make money or for his own personal use. A white man has the idea that since the car is his, he alone should get the benefit from it, but the Guahibo concept is that those who do not own the object should also be served by it.

All Guahibos need to learn both ways of thinking to be able to apply them according to the society within which they find themselves. For example, if a Guahibo were to charge another Guahibo rent for his canoe, it is likely that he will be criticized by other Guahibos, but if he charges rent to a white man, the white man would not be surprised because he is used to doing so himself. So a Guahibo who understands this practice can apply the system he thinks is appropriate, according to the circumstances, since it depends on the culture of the person one is dealing with.

Having cattle is a new experience for the Guahibo people and has caused conflicts among them. But we think it is possible for those who have cattle to share with those who do not or find a way for all to have them so that they can resolve the problem. In that way, no one will be ahead of the rest, and they will not behave like the white people—each one seeking to have only what is his, which in turn causes divisions among them.

A bicycle is a very necessary vehicle, and so it is hoped that everybody will have one of his/her own to avoid the friction caused by lending them. If not, a bicycle owner must lend it based on the person and his/her needs and not to young people who are only going to go on a lark rather than working. But if a bicycle owner sees that there is a real need, he should lend his bicycle to a person who would feel embarrassed should he/she damage it. The same applies to those who own an outboard motor; the borrower should avoid giving rides to people who do not have urgent needs.

School

In order to avoid misunderstandings over school maintenance between parents and primary school bilingual teachers in Guahibo communities, both the parents and the teachers should be given as much guidance as possible, so they can find solutions among themselves, more or less within cultural norms. But to achieve such solutions, it is necessary for the bilingual teachers' superiors to acknowledge that education programs in Guahibo communities should, as much as possible, be within the reach and under the guidance of such communities. When a community has the opportunity of participating in planning their children's education, it will assume greater responsibility in maintaining the school and supporting the bilingual teachers. In that way the teachers' burden will be made lighter and the people will not misinterpret the teachers' attitudes as they work under instructions from their supervisors. Another benefit will be that the townspeople will not go on feeling confused regarding educational and school matters, entirely new experiences for the Guahibo people.

The matter of food distribution by the FER must also be taken into account. The community and its authorities (captains) should be consulted as to the best way to handle it, so it will be properly administered and controlled by all the interested parties, always looking for a mechanism within the culture so that everybody will have a better understanding.

Stores

The stores have caused much misunderstanding among most Guahibos because they do not quite understand their purpose, whether they be communal, private, or those in the missions. So it is important to let the Guahibo people know the purpose of each of these stores. They should know that whoever has a private business is investing his own capital in order to make a profit. He does not think as a Guahibo who has things for the service of all his relatives. Both the one selling and the one buying ought to know this fact. This practice is business in the white man's style, and they can decide if it helps them or not.

People should also understand the purpose of communal stores, which is making a profit for distribution among its associates or for reinvesting in the store and being able to offer more things for sale. Once people understand all of this, they should decide if having a communal store is convenient or not, and if the entire community decides that such a store should go on, they should not allow the managers of it or other people in the community to take advantage of the traditional system to bring an end to the store using the *waquena* system that shares things freely rather than charging a price. For this reason, people should think very carefully about which is best: having to travel long distances to buy a box of matches or having a store in town, even though it is within the white people's system.

Mission store managers rather than other people should be asked if such stores are for profit or if they are intended as an indirect service to the community. That would be a way to clear whatever doubts there might be resulting from rumors in town. Guahibos should know that among whites there are an infinite number of interests and that, therefore, it is not good to believe everything one hears but rather take into account that everyone has his own interests according to how one thinks, the way he lives, and sometimes according to personal conveniences. So one ought to ask first before passing judgment.

Enterprises

It might be that communal enterprises are good for the Guahibo communities, if they are well organized according to Guahibo culture, that is, combining properly traditional values in Guahibo culture and mechanisms from the new (white) economy, so that the enterprise is understood and accepted by the whole community in which it is to be established. But for this combination to work, a very detailed study of the community must be made first.

One should begin by getting to know the prospective enterprise leaders well: to learn if they are conscious of the community needs; to examine their socioeconomic development plans for the community; to find out if they are going to deal honestly with other associates; to see if they are strong enough not to be deceived by people from outside the community; and to see if they are capable people who will not be ensnarled in the capitalist system and lose all interest in their own brothers and in the Guahibo norms. One must be careful to see that the enterprise takes into account the cultural interests of the community where it is going to be established.

Likewise, the people granting loans and providing technical advice to the enterprise must be honest so that they will not deceive the Guahibo people who are not management experts. Such people also should understand and respect the Indian culture.

Furthermore, all associates and their families (the whole community) should be properly instructed in how the enterprise must function, so the community will not impose traditional norms when they should not. They must not only understand how the enterprise functions but must also be of one accord. Everybody should understand how the enterprise leaders are changed whenever a majority of the associates desires.

An enterprise should not abolish the traditional Guahibo idea of the worth of an individual but should rather protect and implement it. Associates should keep the tradition of helping and caring for their fellowmen.

No attempt is being made here to offer solutions to all future Guahibo economic questions but to make only a few suggestions so that the Guahibo people can start orienting themselves and seek to resolve the conflicts they meet without abandoning their own cultural values.

Conclusions

The author wishes to thank all his readers for the time they have spent reading this book. Perhaps they have learned a bit more about how Guahibos think and how their socioeconomic system functions. And hopefully, this knowledge will motivate them to ask themselves how they could be of help to the Guahibo people, how they could show respect for the Guahibo way of thinking, their cultural values, and their human rights. It is the author's hope that Colombian intellectuals should not carry out abstract research, and thus continue hindering the Guahibo peoples' move onward with their own traditional values which have for centuries preserved their harmonious socioeconomic system. The author is profoundly interested in making his own ideas and knowledge known to the honest, highly ethical, intellectual world so that in their future work of investigation they will be able to help the Guahibo people, who until now have had to make all the readjustments in all aspects to be able to survive. Today's Guahibo community, in the face of population increase and their resolve to protect their land, does not feel threatened with disappearance. On the contrary, it hopes that future generations will by all appropriate means defend their own rights to their land and their culture, making sure that their traditional socioeconomic system, which values human beings above material things, should not disappear.

The author wishes to get the attention of the Guahibo youth and tell them that the future of our people depends on them to be the defenders of our good values! All the Guahibo readers of this book should think about this great treasure our people still have, that far from being "savages" as people have called us, we hold on to values that could well serve modern society. We all know that in our traditional economic system having material goods is no reason to undervalue those who do not have them nor is it the case that he who has such things should put a high price on them in times of scarcity. Our system has always been conscience-guided, where everybody values one another because they know that they are all equally valuable.

Epilogue

During the fourteen years since the publication of this book in Spanish in 1985, the Guahibos have maintained their own Guahibo economic system. At the same time, they have learned to function a little more effectively in the national system. At least three new developments have helped them better understand the latter system. In chronological order these are: (1) participation in several cattle projects, (2) participation in local government (at the municipal and state levels), and (3) participation of the indigenous reservations in the national budget. (National funds are forwarded to the municipal government which hands out the money to the reservations according to a plan that the indigenous people present.)

First, the Guahibos have been learning, from several cattle projects in different reservations, how to participate in projects whose principal benefits are for the community. The projects have functioned in spite of certain difficulties. From the difficulties, the Guahibos have continued to learn how to better manage their projects. This author believes that the main benefit of the cattle projects has been what was learned about participation in and administration of development projects. The projects have included aspects of the Guahibo culture such as sharing, and also aspects of the national system, such as profits, evaluations and reports.

Also, the Guahibos are learning to think of the future. With the increase in population in the reservations, the majority are more conscious of the necessity of conserving their natural resources. Although they have not planted palms and other trees, in many reservations they do not sell basic resouces, such as lumber, to the whites but rather save them for their own

117

use. Also, they now have had more practice in defending their lands against squatters.

Second, the Constitution of 1991 provided a basic foundation for the participation of the indigenous communities in the political and economic life of the country. The National Territories were converted into states (departments), and the Guahibos began to participate more in politics representing their people. The indigenous people elected several of their members to the first Vichada state assembly. These people, and others who have been elected to the assembly, the municipal councils, and the mayor's offices, are learning the functions of the administrative and economic systems of the country. Young people studying with white teachers are also learning. Some of the older Guahibos, who have not received an academic orientation, do not yet understand the economic system of the nation, but those that attend the meetings with their politicians and the leaders of their reservations are beginning to learn that orientation.

Sometimes those who do not understand are the authors of rumors, when a leader does not give them "their (personal) part" of a project. In such cases, the leader has to prepare a report and make an evaluation with the people of the project they have requested in order to clear up any misunderstandings. The governors of the reservations are elected for just one year. The majority of the Guahibos now understand the government of their reservations with *cabildos*.

Though the Constitution of 1991 opened the way for the indigenous people of Colombia to participate in politics, the development of indigenous politics in official circles is very difficult, especially in the public entities such as the Senate, the House of Representatives, the state assemblies, and the municipal councils. In the case of the Guahibos, we are few who understand how the whites think and their different way of valuing their economic and human interests. The young Guahibo politicians do not perceive this difference and, in many cases, when they vote for a project, they end up voting against their own interests (those of their community). Beside not understanding the thinking of the nonindigenous people, the Guahibos understand very little of how the rules of a democracy function in regard to decisions that will benefit their people.

Third, based on the Constitution of 1991, there was enacted the Law 80 of 1993, which regulates the annual percentage of funds that each indigenous reservation receives based on the number of inhabitants in the reservation. With this law, the indigenous people began to participate in the government budget. The funds (current income of the nation) arrive at the mayor's office of each municipality. They are distributed to the reservations according to their population, determined by an annual census.

When the governor of the reservation knows the amount of their transfer (of funds), he meets with the captains of the various villages in order to develop a plan for its inversion into projects that the people want. The secretary of the governor writes up the projects, and the governor presents them to the mayor in order to receive the funds. At the end of the year, they prepare an evaluation of how the projects were carried out.

In the state of Vichada, at first the Guahibos only asked for outboard motors and zinc roofing for their houses. With the help of the funds from the transfer, many of the villages now have an outboard motor with the village captain in charge. The person who wants to travel provides the gasoline, and when the motor needs repairs, a collection is taken up in the village.

But the indigenous people have gradually awakened to a new outlook concerning their funds; they are now focusing their use on production rather than only consumer products. In the region where the author lives, the Guahibos now prefer projects that provide help with agriculture, education for young people who want to go on with their studies outside the village, and help for the sick who need to travel to another place for their treatment. With all they have learned, the indigenous people can avoid the problem of the whites continuing to make their decisions for them.

It has been a great challenge for the Guahibos to manage to understand well the function of the official funds as distinct from individual (private) funds. And the author sees that at times there is a great contradiction in the management of the funds because few of the indigenous leaders have understood their administration. Some whites of bad faith have caused some indigenous leaders, who do not understand, to sign receipts for something they do not receive and in this way steal the money. That is, they get the more naive captains or *cabildos* to sign when they should not, and then it looks like the indigenous leaders stole the money, when it is not true.

Also, the whites who are corrupt teach bad ways to the young people and the inexperienced captains. There are some captains and *cabildos* who understand things well and do not operate in bad faith; these men do things right. But there are others who may know better but lend themselves to doing bad things, together with the corrupt whites. In this experience, it can be seen that the majority are very weak and uninformed. Nevertheless, in spite of the failures, the people are learning, and each day they do better and better. Practice is essential, theory alone is insufficient.

The Guahibo politicians, on the other hand, are just beginning to function in party politics and, at the same time, beginning to manage economic funding from the State for social purposes. Since the white politicians are those who deal with social policies, the Guahibo politicians do not know what direction to take as indigenous people. As a result, their white political colleagues direct them toward their own interests. For this reason, the author observes the political process among the Guahibos with much preoccupation because the Guahibo politicians are being directed toward administrative corruption. What is needed is a serious, in-depth analysis of the process in order to determine the best way out for everyone.

For the reader, these comments are to make you aware that the penetration of a different economic system among the Guahibos makes more complex all aspects of the sociopolitical and economic life of this people. The author was an assemblyman for the State of Vichada for two consecutive terms. There he could appreciate and come to know in-depth how the projects are systematized and presented by the whites for their approval. But the Guahibos should not wait expecting others to make decisions for them. The author considers that here are two different ways of thinking concerning economic values. The Guahibo people expect the economy to be distributed to all equally. But for the nonindigenous people the economy is a way of acquiring power and gaining advantage over others. The indigenous people believe that equality produces justice, that justice produces love, and that love produces happiness for all.

It is necessary that the Guahibos understand more deeply the nonindignous system of monetary values so that in the future they can begin to integrate both economies for the benefit of humanity, since it is precisely because of the dollar sign that the nonindigenous people are losing their human dynamism, only because they let themselves be manipulated by personal interests.

Marcelino Sosa, July 1999

Appendix 1

Glossary of Spanish and Guahibo Words

achiote: see *onoto*

amética: a liquid rumored to have power to start an epidemic

araco: a kind of palm tree *(Socratea exorrhiza)* whose wood is used for making bows, shelves, etc.; *macanilla, macana, chuapo*

arrayán: a tree *(Myrtus)* whose bark yields a reddish pigment used to decorate clay pots and paint the inside of gourds

asiwa (Guahibo): to begrudge (things); not sharing; to love (people)

ato (Guahibo): brother

aura (Guahibo): to feel shame, a very deep feeling used among Guahibos to force someone to keep social norms, being self-imposed; it does away with the need for policemen

auríes: mute dogs (*awiri* is 'dog' in Guahibo)

awari (Piaroa): fox

balatá: tree of the *Sapotacea* family, whose latex is used in making chewing gum.

balátuna (Guahibo): plantain

barbasco: several wild and cultivated toxic plants used to poison fish

basue (Guahibo): sugar cane

bole (Guahibo): a bad omen

brillantina: percale cloth

budare: large clay griddle to toast cassava, peppers, etc.

cabildo: legal administrative entity governing Indian reservations from colonial times *cabuya:* string/rope made of palm or other fiber

cafuche: very ferocious wild mammal *(Tayassu pecari)* similar to a hog, found in large herds

cajuche: see *cafuche*

camájita (Guahibo): group hunting or fishing trip lasting several days

capi: a type of vine *(Branisteriopsis caapi)*; Guahibos chew the root bark as a stimulant and hunger killer; shamans also use it as hallucinogen

caribi (Guahibo): a class of spirits

cáyali: red pigment made from a mixture of *onoto* seeds and other substances

concientización: consciousness-raising

cuatro: a musical instrument with four strings like a ukulele

cucurita: palm tree *(Maximiliana sp.)* whose fruit is edible and whose leaves are used in basket weaving and other things

cumare: spiny palm tree *(Astrocaryum chambira)* from whose leaves a much-favored fiber is extracted, young leaves used in hammock weaving, old leaves used in bow-strings, etc.

curare: vine from which dart poison is extracted; the poison

cuyare (Guahibo): necklaces of large glass beads

chiquichique:[16] a palm tree *(Leopoldinia piassava)* whose fiber is used to make brooms and brushes

chuapo: palm tree whose wood is used for house and furniture construction; see *araco*

dacálinae (Guahibo): *pumaroso*, tree whose bark contains a reddish brown pigment used for dyeing thread

dopa (Guahibo): *yopo* powder

dowathi (Guahibo): a class of spirits

dulíacai (Guahibo): type of trap used in fishing

évino (Guahibo): species of yam

finca: farm

fique: pineapple-like plant whose fiber was used to start fires

guahibar: to hunt and/or kill Guahibos

guamo: a branching fruit tree *(Inga sp.)* whose sap is used with charcoal to dye baskets

guapa: shallow, decorated, circular basket used for storing cassava bread and various other purposes

guindos: cords to suspend a hammock

holandilla: fabric for lining

jãjã (Guahibo): yes (affirmative)

---

[16]Since this is a listing of locally-used words in Spanish and Guahibo, the *ch* words appear as the normally would in a Spanish dictionary, after all other words beginning with *c* have been listed.

janibo (Guahibo): state or period of hunger
je je jeee (Guahibo): expression of joy
jiwi (Guahibo): Guahibos, people (Indians or whites)
joropo: type of song sung by plains settlers and cowboys
lapa: spotted cavy, large rodent (*Agouti paca*)
macanilla: see *araco*
maco (Guahibo): mango
mamiri (Guahibo): see *mimbre*
manare: large sifter woven from cane, for sifting cassava flour
mañoco: toasted cassava flour
mapaëto (Guahibo): green pigment made with fruit of *Genipa caruto* tree which turns to indelible black
mapuey: type of yam; see *tabena*
mariscar: hunting or fishing
metsajacobejápano (Guahibo): species of yam
mimbre: the root of an epiphyte plant that is used to tie together the structure of a house, in basket-weaving, etc.; *mamiri* in Guahibo
morichal: stand of *moriche* palms; plural is *morichales*
moriche: a palm tree (*Mauritia flexuosa*) with edible meat covering the nuts, leaves used for roofing houses, and which also provides a fiber used in making *cabuya*, used in weaving hammocks (not as durable as *cumare* palm fiber)
morocota: gold coin (one ounce)
mostacilla: glass beads
no (Guahibo): yam
onoto: plant (*Bixa orellana*) whose seeds are used to make red pigments used as face paint: *achiote*
palo del Brazil: Brazil-wood (*Guilandina [Caesalpinial] echinata*) whose hard, heavy, and compact wood is best for making bows and arrow tips
páwano (Guahibo): species of yam
pecuaino (Guahibo): species of yam
peleguama araguato: material used to make hats
pendare: tree of *Sapotacea* family whose fruit is sweet and edible; the resin is used to make chewing gum and to seal holes in canoe-making
picure: medium-size rodent (*Dasyprocta fulginosa*)
pónajë: (Guahibo): "See you later."
pumaroso: tree (*Bellucia*) whose reddish brown stain is used in dyeing arrow ties; *dacálinae* in Guahibo
punzón: type of fabric
quécoqueco (Guahibo): sticks rubbed together to produce fire
quejee (Guahibo): a shout to announce the catching of a tapir

quérawiri (Guahibo): red pigment obtained by boiling then drying the leaves of a vine *(Arrhabidea chica)*

quiripa: disks made from snail shells perforated to form necklaces which were used as a means of exchange

resguardos: reservations

sabaniar: to scour the savannah in order to find or collect animals

sebucán: cylindrical press of woven cane to extract the juice of the cassava

seje: type of palm from whose nuts oil can be extracted; the nut covering is edible and the Guahibos used the nuts to make a oily "milk"

sesebai (Guahibo): *crown*

tabena: type of edible tuber *(Dioscorea sp.)*

tajamonae (Guahibo): my family

támojo (Guahibo): brother-in-law, male cross-cousin

taxúanë (Guahibo): step-father, uncle-father

topocho: a species of plantain with three-sided fruit

tramojo: a type of leash; tether

troja: a rack for roasting or smoking meat

tsitsito (Guahibo): maraca, gourd rattle

tulíquisi (Guahibo): necklace of small glass beads

tutancán: type of fabric

únuma (Guahibo): cooperative, reciprocal work

urátane (Guahibo): respect or circumspection shown to family members not eligible for marriage, especially mothers-in law and fathers-in law

vegueros: colonists who practice agriculture on the fertile river flood plains

verada: arrow shaft; variety of cane for making arrows

waquena (Guahibo): to show up to claim one's free share of something

wijá (Guahibo): fellow merchants (plural); people used to trading among themselves

wijanë (Guahibo): merchant (singular); client

yáiyatane (Guahibo): respect shown toward authority figures

yaje (Guahibo): a class of spirits

yare: the poisonous juice that comes from the bitter manioc; can be eaten when boiled for a long time

yáwito (Guahibo): a type of trap used in fishing

yona (Guahibo): toxic root used to poison fish (see *barbasco*)

yopo: hardwood tree *(Piptadenia peregrina)*; a hallucinogenic powder is made from the seeds

yucuta: nonfermented drink of cassava and water

Appendix 2

Guahibo Poetry

The author wanted to give other Guahibos an opportunity to express to the readers their own ideas about their culture, particularly about the norms and activities of the Guahibo economy. Each author (including those without any formal education and not very bilingual) wrote originally in Spanish.

The following series of poems were excerpted from *El Pensar Guahibo*, a short publication published by the Guahibo newspaper *La Voz de Cavasi*, 1–4, July and December 1978, July 1979, and July 1981.

Seminomadism

Many Places
When you see something,
When someone dies,
The wife prepares the funeral
To bury him in the home,
To then abandon the Guahibo farm
To go on to start anew in another place.
For this reason Indians have many homes.
      -Luis Pablo Pónare

Summertime
In the summer everybody goes fishing.
They all take along bedding to sleep on the beach.
Sometimes they stay four days,
Some other times a week.
           -Luis Bernardo Pónare

Hunting

The Indian
When dawn comes,
The Indian gets up;
He gives orders to the woman,
"Start up the fire quickly;
I need to get warm
Because I'm going into the woods
Looking for game."
           -Luis Tito Pónare

The Children
Children like to eat meat
Every day.
They pester their father
Until he goes out hunting.
           -Vicente Rodríguez

Hunting
The Indian announces:
"Tomorrow we'll go out *mariscando*,
Brother-in-law, father-in-law,
Uncle, brother."
Next day in the morning
He calls the dogs,
"Tsauto, Calipiri, Murucu,
Aha, aha, aha, aha."
Then they go out into the woods.
Afterwards they find a *lapa*.

The other one says,
"Go up the creek.
Go down the creek."
Then they shoot an arrow at it.
It takes a leap
With a spear in its side
    -Luis Tito Pónare

The *Cajuches*
When the *cajuches* come out,
It could be at any time.
If a Guahibo is hunting in the woods,
If he happens to find the *cajuches*,
He circles around the animals.
He then starts up several fires,
So the animals will not go away.
Then the Guahibo goes out
Running towards the villages.
When he sees the houses from a distance
He right away starts shouting.
He says, "Little brother! Uncle! Granddaddy!
The *cajuches* are coming near."
Then those in the house come out running,
The men, the women, even the children.
They start picking up their bows, arrows, and spears.
The older ones go to guard the *cajuches*.
A woman comes out running to let another community know.
As she leaves the house she starts shouting,
"*Tajamonae* ('family')!
The *cajuches*! Come quickly!"
People from the other village come out with their arrows.
The man says, "Woman, we must take chili, cassava, salt."
    -Luis Tito Pónare

Hunting
To go out hunting,
First you must make a bow
And make arrows and spears.
Afterwards one goes out hunting
In the woods,
Or fishing in the river,
With the same bow.
Then one brings home the game
And cooks it in *yare* with chili.
        -Juan Chipiaje

Hunting
I, when I was small,
Lived with my family.
They taught me to shoot.
I would go into the forest
To know how to follow
Behind the game.
Coming back from the forest,
I would ask my mother,
"How do I change my clothes?"
And she would respond to me,
"The fire is burning.
Get yourself warm
so your clothes will get dry."
        -Luis Tito Pónare

Guahibo Children
Guahibo children,
When they start walking well,
They say, "Dad, make me some arrows,
Because my other playmates have them."
Once the children have their own arrows,
They invent a game.
One of them says, "This is a deer;
This is the tiger, right?
And at the top of this tree
We see the monkey."
They start shooting arrows
To see if they manage to hit something.
"How good it is to shoot!"
The Guahibo children say.
       -Luis Tito Pónare

The Dog
The dog says,
"I'm a good hunter,
But I have no wife.
My wife left me
With another dog;
The dog's name's Chipolo.
My wife's name was Chucuta.
When I had a wife,
I would kill any animal:
Lapa, deer, wild boar, *picure*.
Now I can no longer hunt
Because nobody cleans the game.
I do my own cooking
When I bring home some game,
But now I feel lazy
To prepare food,"
Says the hunting dog.
       -Luis Pablo Pónare

Footprint
On a Sunday
The Guahibos get together.
The village captain says,
"Tomorrow we must go tapir-hunting."
Then they all go out into the woods.
They go on the trail,
And find a footprint.
The chief goes up front.
"*Jājā*, a tapir went this way.
But this footprint is two days old."
Everybody looks at it:
"Yes, it is two day's old."
Further on they find another footprint.
They say, "Today it passed by here.
It must be in this brush.
We should all surround the brush."
Then they pick one from among them.
"You go and follow the footprints
until you find it."
When the man finds the tapir,
He shouts:
"*Metsaja ra liabooo.*
Metsaja ra liabooo.
Metsaja ra labooo."
Meaning 'There goes the tapir'.
With the shout
He lets them know,
Those who are waiting.
      -Luis Tito Pónare

The Animals' Footprints

A Guahibo goes out into the woods
Looking for game, and sees
The footprint of a tapir or of a deer.
Right away he concentrates
Thinking to find out
How long ago the animal had
Been in that place,
Or how long it has been since
It has gone by.
A Guahibo can always recognize
Animal footprints.
He knows how to estimate
By a footprint's decomposition
If it has been a short time ago
Or it has been a long time ago
That the animal passed by,
And this depends on the condition
Of the soil,
The action of the temperature,
Rain, etc.
He calculates the effect of these forces
Also on the broken branches.
That way he more or less knows
How far the game is.
For this reason a Guahibo
Thinks a child should go out
With him so he can teach him
The forces that affect footprints
And that way learn more
To be able to fend for himself
In his own environment.
      -Marcelino Sosa

Fishing

Summer
In the summertime
An Indian gets up early.
The sun is coming up.
He says, "*Je je jee.*"
Then the Indian says,
"Today will be a good day for fishing.
Wife, take cassava, matches;
Take chili also to eat
With roasted fish."
    -Luis Tito Pónare

Yona
In summertime,
When he did not yet know a fishing hook,
Indians used to fish with *yona*.
One digs out *yona* roots,
One crushes it with a log,
Then one casts it into a creek,
Or a lake, or a pond, or a river.
One takes the fish out of the lake.
One has a *troja* ready
On which to roast the fish.
Then after it is roasted,
The following day,
One grinds the fish.
This ground fish
Can be kept a long time.
    -Luis Alberto Quintero Sosa

Gathering

When We Lack Something
When we have no oil,
We think of something
With which to light the house.
So we go into the woods
To get sap from the trees.
We bring the sap home;
We boil it.
Then we take some rags;
We place the rags into the sap;
Then it becomes like a candlestick.
With that stick we light the house.
        -Luis Tito Pónare

The Ants
The month of May is ant season.
They start flying at noon.
The women are ready,
Each one with her pot.
They can tell time without a watch.
When it's time for the ants to start flying,
They take off their good clothes.
Then they start catching
The ants that are going to fly away.
        -Juan Luis Chipiaje

Work

A Guahibo Woman's Work
She works in the manioc patch.
She also twists *cabuya* fiber
For making hammocks.
She never rests.
If she's home,
She finishes up the *cabuya* ball;
She twists more for the hammock handles.
She works more than a man,
All summer long,
All winter long,
Because she doesn't know
How to count weeks.
She only rests
On the day she twists *cabuya*.
      -Juan Selzo Chipiaje

Money
Indians like
To work every year,
But they never think
About money-making.
      -Vicente Rodríguez

Working Together
When they are going to do a job,
The job's owner
Has to prepare food
For many people.
He goes to the garden
In the afternoon
To get the food ready.
Next day the people come
Just before sunrise
Ready to work.
In the owner's home
Each person gets
His share of food.

If it is fish or wild meat,
The workmen are very happy
Because they ate meat.
Then they sharpen their tools
And say goodbye.
They say, "*pónajë*,"
Meaning 'see you later'.
In the afternoon they come back from work.
They all go home.
One of them says, "I am very tired.
Many chiggers."
Another one says the same thing.
Now the owner owes one day's work
To all who worked for him.
That is how Guahibos are.
>   -Luis Tito Pónare

Women

Women work all day long
Baking cassava bread for the children.
They first pull out the manioc tubers;
Then they peal and grate them,
And leave the dough.
The following day they make cassava bread
In the hot plate
Made of mud.
>   -Pedro José Chipiaje

Sweethearts

The young man began to know life.
So he fell in love with a girl.
He starts helping the girl's father
Since he already can work.
The boy always comes to help with the work.
Then the girl's father and mother say,
"I think he is coming for you."
Then they send her to feed him.
That way they keep falling in love

Until they get married.
Then the young man
Has to live close to the father-in-law
And helps him with the work.
He has to bring game and fish.
An Indian's courtship is very different
From that of white people.
        -Tito Pónare

Cassava Bread
If a woman makes cassava bread,
She first pulls out bitter manioc.
She grates it into the dough container.
The following day she takes a *sebucán*
And squeezes the juice out of the dough.
Then she mashes and strains it,
And makes the cassava bread in the *budare*.
        -Jorge Tovar

The Garden
To make a garden
People go into the woods
Looking for good soil.
Then they clear the underbrush.
After that they cut down the trees.
Then they leave it alone for one month
Or six weeks.
Then they burn it up.
They plant bitter manioc,
Sweet manioc, cane, yams,
Plantains, and chili peppers.
They plant rice and corn.
That is how Indians work
In summertime.
        -Campo Elías Sosa

The House

The Beds
Guahibo beds
Have no mattresses;
Their beds are
Made of *cumare* palm.
First they extract the fiber,
Then they twist it.
After that they weave hammocks.
Then they make hammock ropes or: *guindos*
To hang them.
Guahibos do not sleep on the ground;
That is what they make hammocks for.
    -Alejo Pérez

The Office
The *La Voz de Cavasi* office
Has a thatch roof
Of *moriche* palm leaves.
First the frame poles were cut
And tied up with vines.
Then they split palm strips,
Tied them to the frame
And put the palm leaves on top.
This roof will last five years.
    -Alejo Pérez

Sharing

How We Share
A Guahibo goes out into the forest
Looking for game.
After many hours
Of walking through the woods,
He finds something, like a boar
Or two wild turkeys.
Once he kills the game,
He must think on how to share the meat
With the other families.

On his way back home,
He is very happy.
Those who stayed home
Step out looking every moment
To see when he comes with the game.
When they see him coming far away,
They start shouting,
"The hunter is coming!
He is bringing some game!"
Right away they start a fire,
So it will be ready.
When he comes into the house,
The children say,
"A hunk of ribs for me."
Another one asks for the part he wants.
Such is the Guahibos' life.
They are used to sharing.
   -Luis Tito Pónare

In The Afternoon
People are starting to come back
From felling trees
To make gardens.
The wife prepares the food.
The man comes home and
He says to the woman, Watuliba,
"Pull out the table and benches."
Then he starts calling out,
"*Ato* (brother), *tamojo* (brother-in-law)..."
And everybody starts coming in.
One of them says,
"This fish with chili
Is very tasty."
Then they start laughing
Because Indians cannot eat alone.
When they eat alone,
Without their relatives,
They feel uncomfortable
Within themselves.
How nice my Guahibo culture is!
   -Luis Tito Pónare

Trading

A Female Dog
I have a good female dog.
This dog chases *cajuche*,
Boar, armadillo, tapir.
I bought this dog
For an ax, and arrow, a spear,
A machete, an old cooking pot
(because I did not have a new one).
I still owe
A jar of ground chili;
I owe a belt,
I owe a shirt,
No more.
This dog's name is Tulica
      -Vicente Rodríguez

A Brazil Bow
In Guahibo culture,
To make a good bow,
They first look for Brazil wood.
In the middle of the forest
This kind of wood is found.
One day they get together
Several people and say,
"Tomorrow let us go looking
For Brazil wood."
Another one says, "I am going too.
I do not have a bow."
They take food for the trip,
So they will be able to stay
Three or five days in the woods,
Cutting down and splitting wood.
On their way back home,
They go loaded down,
Each piece weighs fifteen pounds,
And so each of them carries
Six pieces.
They hike two whole days.
When they get home,

Others come in and
One of them asks,
"How much is each piece?
Do you need a spear or some chili?"
Another one says, "I have a piece
In exchange for a shirt."
He answers him, "I have no shirt,
Only a jar of good chili."
That is how Indians do business.
A Brazil bow is very fine,
But also very heavy.
When it falls in a pond
Or in a river,
The bow is lost
Because Brazil wood is very heavy.
It sinks.
Each person has a bow,
Even the seven-year-olds
Have bow and arrows
And know how to shoot.
          -Luis Pablo Pónare

References

Coppens, Walter. 1971a. La tenencia de tierra indígenas en Venezuela, Aspectos legales y antropológicos. Antropológica 29:1–37.

———. 1971b. "Las relaciones comerciales de los Yekuana del Caura-Paragua. Antropológica 30:28–59.

del Rey Fajardo, José, S. J. 1971. Aportes jesuítieas a la filología colonial venezolana, Toma II. Caracas: Universidad Católica Andrés Bello.

Eden, Michael J. 1974. Ecological aspects of development among Piaroa and Guahibo Indians of the Upper Orinoco basin. Antropológica 39:25–56.

Gumilla, P. Jose, S. J. 1955. El Orinoco ilustrado, edición de la Presidencia de Colombia. Bogotá: Editorial ABC.

Kirchoff, Paul. 1948. Food gathering tribes of the Venezuelan Llanos: The Guahibo and Chiricoa. Handbook of South American Indians. Washington, D.C.: Smithsonian Institute.

Kondo, Riena W. 1973. Guahibo. In Aspectos de la Cultura Material de Grupos Etnicos de Colombia I:195–213. Lomalinda, Colombia: Instituto Lingüístico de Verano.

La Voz de Cavasi (Cavasilivaisi). 1978.

Lucena Salmoral, Manuel. 1970–71. Notas sobre la magia de los guahibos. Revista Colombiana de Antropología, XV:129–69.

Méndez, Eustorgio. 1970. Los principales mamíferos de silvestres de Panamá. Panamá: Private edition.

Morey, Robert V. 1979. A joyful harvest of souls: Disease and the destruction of the Llanos Indians. Antropológica 52:77–108.

————— and Nancy Morey. 1975. Relaciones comerciales en el pasado en los Llanos de Colombia y Venezuela. Montalbán UCAB 4:533–64.

Patiño, Víctor Manuel. 1977. Recursos naturales y plantas útiles en Colombia, aspectos históricos. Bogotá: Instituto Colombiano de Cultura.

Pérez Arbeláez, Enrique. 1956. Plantas útiles de Colombia. Bogotá: Librería Colombia.

Reyes Posada and Alejandro Clemencia Chiappe de Reyes. 1973. Los Guahibos hoy. Informe de la región de Planas, DIGIDEC 3. Bogotá: Ministerio de Gobierno, Dirección General de Integración y Desarrollo de la Comunidad.

Rivera, José Eustacio. 1981. La Vorágine. México: Editores Mexicanos Unidos. (First published in 1925.)

Rivero, P. Juan, S.J. 1956. Historia de las misiones de los Llanos de Casanare y los Ríos Orinoco y Meta. Bogotá: Biblioteca de la Presidencia de Colombia.

Sosa, Marcelino. 1979. El guahibo y el blanco (culturas en conflicto). Bogotá: Ministerio de Gobierno.

—————. 1983. El niño guahibo y la educación bilingüe. Bogotá: private edition.

Vélez Boza, Fermín and Juan Baumgartner. 1962. Estudio general, clínico y nutricional en tribus indígenas del territorio federal Amazonas de Venezuela. Archivos Venezolanos de Nutrición. XII:143–225.

www.ingramcontent.com/pod-product-compliance
Lightning Source LLC
Chambersburg PA
CBHW062037270326
41929CB00014B/2460